meditations *for* new moms

meditations
for
new moms

Reflections, Scripture, and Wisdom
for Mommy's First Year

SANDRA DRESCHER-LEHMAN

Good Books®
New York, New York

Good Books books may be purchased in bulk at special discounts
for sales promotion, corporate gifts, fund-raising, or educational
purposes. Special editions can also be created to specifications.
For details, contact the Special Sales Department, Good Books,
307 West 36th Street, 11th Floor, New York, NY 10018 or
info@skyhorsepublishing.com.

Good Books is an imprint of Skyhorse Publishing, Inc.®, a Delaware
corporation.

Visit our website at www.goodbooks.com.

10 9 8 7 6 5 4 3 2 1

Library of Congress Cataloging-in-Publication Data is available on file.

Cover design by Laura Klynstra
Cover photo courtesy of iStock/gianliguori

Print ISBN: 978-1-68099-129-1
Ebook ISBN: 978-1-68099-140-6

Printed in China

Dedicated to Maria Dawn and Jonathan Brooks,
our children, who have given me
new definitions for birth, life, and love.

About This Book

When I became a new mother, I learned to know many new sides of myself. I discovered new coping skills, new limits, new definitions for love and anger, new companionship with God. During the first year of my daughter Maria's life, and then again after my son Jonathan was born, I experienced joy that soared to new heights and emotional dips that went lower than I had previously known. I was grateful for the friends who continually assured me of my worth as a mother by listening to my various emotions without condemnation.

My hope is that you will find a friend who validates your experiences in the first year of motherhood, whether it's with your first child or your sixth. The agony of a hard day or week decreases as you admit how bad it feels, and joy is multiplied as you share it.

These meditations are short, in keeping with the amount of time you have to yourself as a new mother. They also offer a prayer, an action, or a suggestion for thought that you can take with you into the living of your day. My hope is that we will all be better mothers and women as we listen to ourselves, each other, and God.

—Sandra Drescher-Lehman

Sensual Nourishment

The world has never felt or looked, sounded, smelled, or tasted so wonderful as it does today. I'm in it like the newborn I hold, and everything is refreshing, invigorating!

Did the birds just start to sing outside my bedroom window? Where did the yellow dandelions get their brilliance? Have strawberries always tasted this sweet? The air itself smells new, as if it were blown in special delivery to welcome my baby and her now mother. It nudges me gently with a shy kiss before it's off to play in the old maple tree. The arrival of my baby has renewed my senses, as if it is I who's just been born!

**Join your baby
by taking the invitation to a new life.**

O Lord, our Sovereign,
how majestic is your name in all the earth.
—Psalm 8:1

1

Amazing

His fingers are so tiny!
My hand covers half his body.

I can hardly imagine that he has all the parts of an adult body in his tiny parcel!

His skin is liquid soft.

I'm vaguely aware that I am babbling all those obvious things that sound so silly when other people say them! At the same time, I can't quit. It's as if I must announce the profundity of this event and this baby to the world—and even to myself.

This baby is a true miracle.

**Let your babbling
be your prayer.**

I praise you,
for I am fearfully and wonderfully made.
—Psalm 139:14

Power

I feel incredibly powerful.

My body still aches from the labor of bringing this child to her first view of the world. I move slowly, and I sleep whenever possible, but in my mind I have suddenly leaped to a position of power. I have entered a new realm of womanhood—a woman who is also Mother.

This fragile child depends on me for everything. I am responsible for all her needs. I am her most natural connection with her Creator. She will know God's love through mine. She will experience God's tenderness through my touch. And I will regain the physical part of my power as God carries both of us.

**God, help me to enjoy the power
you have given me, without abusing it.**

Those who wait for the Lord shall renew their strength,
they shall mount up with wings like eagles,
they shall run and not be weary,
they shall walk and not faint.

—Isaiah 40:31

Commitment

Before I was out of the recovery room, I called my parents. Before I was able to stand alone, they were kissing my weary smile. Before I was back home, they were fixing my meals and bed. I am thirty-six years old and just as much their child as ever.

This little one in my arms is mine forever, too! I won't quit being her mother when she turns eighteen or leaves home or has her own family or . . . ever for the rest of my life!

What have I done?

**Thank God,
I am not alone.**

You are my Lord;
I have no good apart from you.

—Psalm 16:2

Changing Lifestyle

I never dreamed my world could be so revolutionized! Last month I did whatever I wanted to do, whenever I wanted to do it, for the most part. I could follow through on my plans. I was dependable.

This month I am controlled by this squirming, demanding eight-pounder. I am late for everything. I no longer go out for coffee on a whim. It takes me all day to get myself into the shower, and then it's a quickie. Sometimes I can't even get to the phone on time!

I had decided this baby would not change my life. That was definitely a pre-birth luxury decision. Why didn't somebody warn me about this lifestyle modification?

Well, I'm learning it now. Actually, change can be intriguing. My attitude determines whether I resist it or welcome it.

**God, help me to accept my new limitations
and receive this as new stimulation.**

. . . the faithfulness of the Lord endures forever!
—Psalm 117:2

Storytelling

My poor mother. I'm suddenly pounding her with questions about what happened over thirty years ago.

Alter I had been at work all day, my nameless baby kept me up all night before he finally made his debut at 6 a.m. Now I want to know when I was born and how long we were in labor.

He was a huge eight pounds, four ounces, a fact I continue to be reminded of every time I sit down. I want to know how big I was, and what I looked like, and how soon she knew what my personality would be, and what my doctor was like, and how much Dad was involved with my birth, and on and on.

Strange how oblivious I was to all those things before and how important they suddenly are now. Stories are the connection to my past and my present, and they will prepare me for the future. Storytelling will have to be my next vocation!

**Ask to hear the stories
from your baby days.**

And [Jesus] told them many things in parables,
saying, "Listen . . . I."

—Matthew 13:3

Memories

My mother was wise. She didn't give me any of my baby memoirs—books, pictures, clothes, blankets, or cards—until my baby was born. She knew I wouldn't have appreciated them before. In fact, I never missed them!

Now they are the most precious gifts she could give. I go from tears to giggles and back again, looking through these treasures and reading what she wrote about me.

Motherhood is not the only new stage I'm entering. I'm also being re-mothered by the memories of how I was first mothered when I was too tiny to remember.

**How are you preserving
the memories of your baby?**

His mother used to make for him a little robe
and take it to him each year.
—I Samuel 2:19

All-Encompassing Love

As John and I have grown closer during the eight years of our marriage, I have become convinced that I could never love anyone as much as I love him. Suddenly, however, I have a new depth of love that is unfamiliar and glorious at the same time! How did it get here? John and I have worked and worked at our love, yet my love for this child has simply been a gift.

Maybe the maternal instinct is a reality after all! My baby's dependence on me is totally endearing. I've never had anyone need me this much. It feels like time has stopped and this baby I hold is my whole life.

**Envision love
flowing through you like a river.**

Love never ends.
—I Corinthians 13:8

Birth

With her first breath, I lost mine. As she wiggled out of control into her new space, I froze in awe. Her screams pierced my anticipation, triggering my tears of relief. Her vulnerability and trust followed her into our world.

Her mouth searched for a place to suck. My body, full and waiting, filled it. At last she looked up to meet her mother. Our spirits joined, and I knew that life would never be the same again.

Thank you, God.
Thank you, God.

[God] gives breath
to the people upon [the earth]
and spirit to those who walk in it.
—Isaiah 42:5

Pregnant No More

I miss being pregnant! I could hardly wait for this baby to be born so I could sleep on my stomach again and sleep without being suddenly kicked awake. I was eager to cuddle the baby in my arms, count its fingers and toes, tie my own shoes again, etc., etc.

But now I feel empty. My secret is gone. This baby seems different from the baby I carried within me for nearly nine months. That hidden mystery, which grew along with my feelings of being co-creator with God, was suddenly born.

Now everyone can see when he moves. He sleeps in another room. I go out and strangers no longer know there's another part of me at home.

My heart yearns for the familiar unknowing of pregnancy.

**Mourn the loss,
but let your heart also respond
with joy to the one
who now cries for your continuing vigilance.**

The time came for [Mary]
to deliver her child.

—Luke 2:6

Visitors

My grandpa found a nice way to get rid of visitors who overstayed their welcome. He would bring out the guest book and say, "We'd like you to sign this now before you leave."

Well, I need a guest book! It's nice to have friends stop by and meet my new daughter. But when they sit here and look at her for three hours, and I feel like I have to entertain them, I lose my happy mood. I can tell the ones who have had children. They're in and out in five minutes, a breath of fresh air that still smells sweet when they're gone. The others, well, it's hard for me to eke out, "Thanks for coming," when they finally leave.

My mother was here to protect me the first week. She always thought of some polite way to let people know their visit was appreciated and that they were free to go! I guess I'll have to start speaking up for my own needs.

**Repeat to yourself as many times as necessary:
"The baby and I come first right now."**

Well meant are the wounds a friend inflicts.

—Proverbs 27:6

Exhausted

I have never been this tired before in my life—at least not for this long. I've felt worn out after a race or after biking up a mountain, but it was nothing a big dinner and good night of sleep couldn't fix.

But this is ridiculous! I feel like I could sleep forever; I can't imagine ever having energy again. No one told me it would take so much life out of me to have a baby!

It makes sense. These bodies, my baby's and mine, have definitely been traumatized. She seems to know what she needs to do about it—she just eats and sleeps. She doesn't even bother smiling at anyone.

I could learn something here.

**Treat your body to what it deserves—
good food and "Good night."**

He gives sleep
to his beloved.

—Psalm 127:2

Nursing

How did this infant, barely out of her cozy womb, know how to suck when I offered my nipple? How did she know it was her responsibility, now, to receive nourishment through her lips, after all that time of passive growth?

And how did my body know it was time to start producing milk? It just started working, on schedule, yielding the needed nutrition.

I know the right answers. God created us both to work this way. That sounds so simple, yet the reality is so complex and amazing. I find myself just watching her. We are both part of God's miracle and are incredibly blessed.

**Thank you, Creator,
for your intricate blending
of our needs and gifts.**

"Blessed are you among women,
and blessed is the fruit of your womb."

—Luke 1:42

Precious

Something about the smell of my baby stirs unnamed memories from my subconscious. It creates images of fresh innocence, the preciousness of her life that fills my head to include all of life. It provokes dreams about the absence of evil and about the peaceful order God first created for the world. It invites the awe of new beginnings back into my imagining and places the reality of my charge in the center of my heart.

I can't get enough of it. My nose finds her neck again and takes another deep breath.

**Let your sense of smell
talk to you of life.**

Your anointing oils are fragrant,
your name is perfume poured out.
—Song of Solomon 1:3

Gender Disappointment

It seems like a heresy of motherhood to admit this, but I am not miraculously bonding with my baby. Everyone assured me it would happen instantly, so what's wrong with me?

It's not that I don't love him, or that I'm not grateful for this precious healthy son, but now I know that I really wanted a girl. I always thought he was a girl! I even had some cute little dresses ready to wear on this baby. I called him "her" all the way through my pregnancy, and I still say "she" sometimes when I'm talking about him.

It's an embarrassing attitude, but denying it wouldn't help either, because I'm carrying it right here within me.

Thank you, God,
for understanding my disappointment.
Nurture my love for my son.

Great is our Lord,
and abundant in power;
his understanding is beyond measure.
—Psalm 147:5

Gender Joy

Acknowledging my disappointment about having a boy instead of a girl gave me the courage to tell my husband how I feel. He didn't condemn me, but I could tell he didn't share my feelings. In fact, a smile softened his whole face as he talked about having a son, someone with whom to share "male things"! He holds Jonathan with such gentleness and looks at him with eyes that see the possibilities of all they will do and be together.

A deep satisfaction builds within me as I watch the bonding of father and son. Maybe it's the beginning of my own power to bond.

Let go of the drive to be all things to your baby, and continue to let the love of others in.

As a father has compassion for his children,
so the Lord has compassion for those who fear him.
—Psalm 103:13

Insecure

I keep telling myself that every new job feels like this. I don't know what I'm doing! Whatever possessed me to think I could learn to do it? I wonder why I didn't stay where I was, where I knew my routine and could function without having to think through every move so carefully.

On the other hand, I like the excitement of new challenges; I've always eventually learned to feel comfortable with new jobs. Motherhood is following my previous pattern of initial job insecurity. I hope the increased comfort level follows with time as well!

**Think of yourself as a young plant
as you begin this new job of mothering.
Open your tender shoots
to God's nurturing showers.**

You shall be like a watered garden,
like a spring of water, whose waters never fail.
—Isaiah 58:11

Awesome

It's an amazing activity to watch. When I see her mouth open like a baby bird, assuming food will be forthcoming, I know the child development theories are right: babies make no distinction between themselves and their mothers.

Sometimes I don't make the distinction myself! After living so connected for nine months and remaining dependent on each other after birth, I feel like I'm in a tight circle with her. No one can break into it, and we don't want to break out of it.

Soon enough other demands will enter for both of us. For now, however, I will relish the beauty with which we are creating and helping each other to grow. I will let our circle float in the warm bubble of God's love.

**How has your
baby nurtured your soul?**

Out of the mouths of infants and nursing babies
you have prepared praise for yourself.
—Matthew 21:16

Baby's Development

Newborns can best focus their sight on an object twelve inches from their eyes. They cannot see something closer or farther away until they are older. They especially like to look at black and white objects in the first months, and at facial features.

I don't know who figured that out, but it's easy to believe. When I cradle my baby in my arms and he looks up at me from that magic distance, he looks content. He studies me like it's his job to do, which I guess it is! He feels relaxed in my arms.

I thought I'd get a lot of reading done in those hours as I hold him while he drinks. Most of the time, though, I find myself just gazing at his face, reading it and watching him read mine. I can tell the development of his vision is no accident. Someone planned it perfectly.

**Imagine being held by God
in the same tenderness
with which you hold your baby.
Let God's face of steadfast love shine on you.**

Let your face shine upon your servant;
save me in your steadfast love.

—Psalm 31:16

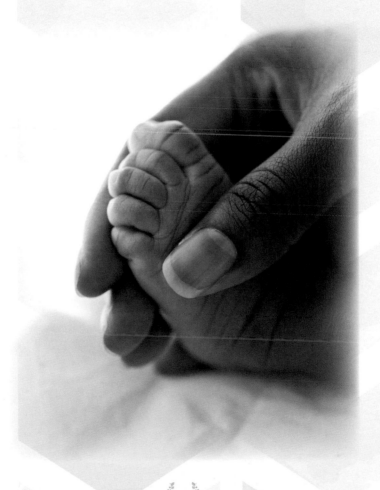

Career Mother

Before I was a mother, I would have come close to agreeing with this concluding verse from Ecclesiastes: "There is nothing better for mortals than to eat and drink, and find enjoyment in their toil." I thought of my work as a gift from God. It gave me enjoyment, let me serve others, and paid the bills. I planned to take off several weeks to be with my baby, regain my energy, and fit back into my clothes. After that it would be back to work for this woman!

Suddenly, however, it's not so simple. No one else can take care of this baby and love her like I can. She needs me. I don't want to leave her! My careful plans for the future have been shattered with her arrival into this world where I can see her and hold her in my arms.

I need to decide all over again if I will work in or away from my home and how I will handle the emotions of either choice.

**God, help lend your wisdom
to balance my emotions.**

There is nothing better for mortals than to eat
and drink, and find enjoyment in their toil.
—Ecclesiastes 2:24

Memory Loss

I've always been a list person, keeping track on my over-sized calendar of all I have to do. But this is ridiculous. Just when I need to be most organized to handle all these new responsibilities, I even forget to write things down!

It's disconcerting to be this unorganized and undependable. I'd rather have the pregnant clumsies again than feel this postpartum stupidity. Maybe my body's trying to tell me to forget the external for a while. Come to think of it, I haven't needed a list to take care of my baby.

**God, help me
to trust and listen
to my body.**

. . . a time to break down,
and a time to build up.
—Ecclesiastes 3:3

Mother to Mother

I've already lost track of how many diapers I've changed. While I was pregnant, I imagined that would be the worst job of mothering. But I'm amazed at how, even when he squirts me in the face, I love making him dry and smell good again. Sometimes it's inconvenient, though, and I think it's a shame he won't remember all I'm doing for him in these first years.

Then I'm amazed that my mother never threw that in my face when I was an ungrateful teenager. She never asked me to help her in return for all the diapers she had changed for me.

I never realized, before, what all she *has* done for me. I have a new love and respect for her, now that I'm beginning to get a glimpse of the work of mothering. I was loved deeply before I knew the word, and that love is now mine to pass on and instill in this tiny infant, whether or not he ever thinks about how many of his diapers I've changed.

Write your mother a note of appreciation for what she gave you before you were old enough to know.

And she gave birth to her firstborn son
and wrapped him in bands of cloth,
and laid him in a manger.

—Luke 2:7

C-Section

A good friend called yesterday to share the news of a baby girl born to her the previous week. It was not the usual joyous birth call, however. She had been rushed to the hospital for an emergency C-section. Her husband, who had anticipated his role as coach throughout all their childbirth classes, sat helpless in the waiting room, dependent on strangers for any news.

Fortunately the baby is fine, but my friend's dreams of how she would give birth were dashed. The pain of surgery has greatly decreased the comfort of holding her baby. The fear and vulnerability of those hours altered the joy she had anticipated. Doing it alone was a huge disappointment for both her and her husband.

I pray that she will eventually know that she offered all the love and knowledge she could possibly give.

**O God,
heal our broken dreams.**

The Lord is your keeper.
The Lord is your shade at your right hand.
—Psalm 121:5

Mother Identity

I'm a mother! Yesterday someone referred to me as a mother. That's also what the hospital papers said of me. Every time the word "Mother" connects itself with me, something in the center of my being flutters around like my baby is still inside.

I wonder what all it will mean. I wonder how many diapers it means I'll change, how many Band-Aids I'll put on, how many kisses and hugs I'll exchange.

This is all uncharted territory—at least by me! Untold women have undertaken this vocation before. I've read their stories. Nothing, however, prepared me for this sudden awareness, that I am now one of them!

I'm sort of glad babies don't arrive talking. Maybe by the time she learns to say, "Mama," I'll be able to receive it with joy instead of shock.

**Look in a mirror and hear God say to you,
"You are a beautiful mother."**

The man named his wife Eve,
because she was the mother of all living.
—Genesis 3:20

Postpartum Depression

I feel like crying. I don't even know why exactly. I just know my eyes are floodgates—sometimes holding back the tears, and unable to do so at other times.

I could blame it on a lack of sleep: namely, exhaustion. I could blame it on my changing hormones. Sometimes that's heartening; other times it's just plain disgusting. Why does my body have so much power over me?

I guess my hormones *are* me right now, though. Somehow, when I read about others' experiences with postpartum depression, I figured I could live above that. I'm a strong woman, after all. Besides, I wanted this baby. How could I get so depressed that one look at her cherub face wouldn't cheer me right up?

But I still feel like crying.

**Thank you, God,
for accepting my tears as easily as my joy.**

I am weary with my moaning:
every night I flood my bed with tears.
—Psalm 6:6

Expansion

During my pregnancy, I was amazed by how much my body could stretch to make room for a growing baby. Now that he's out here with me all the time, I'm thinking that was the easy part!

Now my head has to expand to think for two. My muscles have to grow stronger to hold him. I have to make more physical space available in the house for the arrival of toys, a crib, diapers, and clothes. Even my social contacts are multiplying with my new membership in the world of mothers.

Help me, Lord,
to accept the expansion
my baby brings to my whole world,
In the same awe and joy
with which I watched my belly grow.

The Lord
will keep your going out and your coming in
from this time on and forevermore.

—Psalm 121:8

God as Parent

This baby, small and silent, is already having a huge effect on my belief system. She weighs less than two bags of sugar, but she has all the same parts as I do! She lies here unable to do anything for herself, and yet I value her more highly than anything I have ever known. She does nothing to earn my love, and yet I love her more than I ever knew of love. She's completely dependent on me for nourishment, protection, and a dry bottom. How vulnerable! How utterly exposed and beautiful!

Maybe, just maybe, God loves me, too, for just being. Maybe my independence and accomplishments are not as precious to God as they have become to me. Maybe my value also comes in my vulnerable stillness, taking refuge in the arms of my Creator.

**Be still
and know you are loved.**

How precious is your steadfast love, O God!
All people may take refuge in the shadow of your wings.
—Psalm 36:7

Simple Joys

Today a friend asked me what my baby is doing new this week. What a delightful question! I wanted to tell everyone that he rolled over for the first time and that I'm sure his smile was meant for me, and that he reached out to the dog for the first time. But I didn't really expect to find anyone interested enough to listen. I'm too afraid of being written off as one of those doting parents who bores everyone.

But I love to watch his every new expression; his every discovery of how another body part works; his interest every time he touches a new toy. I am suddenly able, in a new way, to recognize the simple beauty around me. Perhaps God, as parent, delights in all my new little discoveries, too.

**God, help me to receive my whole world
the same way I watch for my baby's discoveries
with anticipation and celebration!**

Truly I tell you,
whoever does not receive the kingdom of God
as a little child will never enter it.

—Luke 18:17

First Smile

My baby smiled at me today and all time stopped. Her face lit my whole world! I was in the middle of reading about all the dangers to an infant that lurk in the home, but I had to stop and respond to this radiance beside me. My worries no longer existed. My fear melted into a warm blur of nothingness. All I could do was to watch her in awe, hoping to see that beautiful smile again, and to sit in the glow of what she had already given. I smiled back, then laughed in the pure joy of such wonderful communication.

They say a smile can be given in any language. Today I think she did it in every language at the same time. I'm a rich person for having received the gift of that smile. My baby's!

**Thank you, God,
for showering me with your joy
through my baby's smile.**

For you, O Lord,
have made me glad by your work;
at the works of your hands I sing for joy.
—Psalm 92:4

Co-Creator

I have never felt so connected to God, creator of my own intricate body and now using mine to create another. God has not chosen to create alone since that first person centuries ago. I was needed, too, for this miracle to be conceived and birthed.

As far as I can tell, God didn't forget anything in my formation. (Well, I was missing one wisdom tooth, but that only saved me from getting one more removed!) It looks like our baby is also formed in perfection.

With each new child, it appears God still does most of the work of creation. How like God, though, to let me feel needed in this process, too. I am humbled and exalted at the same time in our partnership.

**Imagine a slow-motion movie
of your inward parts
being lovingly formed.**

For it was you
who formed my inward parts.

—Psalm 139:13

Love . . . Gifts

Every time I walk into, or past, a store these days, I see things I want to buy for the baby. It's not really a sensible desire to meet her needs. I want to buy her the cute blanket I see, even though she already has too many to use. I have an urge to stock up at the sale on baby wipes, although I know there are already three containers in the closet! She didn't even know how to rip the paper off all those Children's Day presents I got for her.

Sometimes I imagine God being this to me—a loving and, yes, even doting parent, always wanting to give to me, too. "God is love" is suddenly more than the first verse I learned as a child.

**Repeat "God is love"
as you think about all the gifts surrounding you.**

If you then . . .
know how to give good things to your children,
how much more will your Father in heaven
give good things to those who ask Him!
—Matthew 7:11

Lonely

I feel so lonely today! Even though I have plenty to do, there's a vague emptiness in the center of my body. It rears its head to be noticed, but won't come close enough to be named.

In my head I know there are lots of other women in the world having their first baby right now, too, but in my gut, I feel like I'm the only one. I'm inexperienced and incompetent, dragged out of the office into a diaper pail. No wonder no one has followed me.

Help! Save me from myself.

Thank you, Lord.
I just noticed your hand.

I have taken you
by the hand
and kept you.

—Isaiah 42:6

Love

Being a mother has suddenly cast a wonderful and sometimes strange light on how I think about those who had a role in my creation—my father, my mother, God. I knew they loved me, but I never knew love could be as profound as that which I feel for this baby of mine. I knew they thought about my welfare, but I didn't understand, before, how comprehensive those thoughts were in all they did.

I knew it was hard to let me move out on my own, but I already cannot imagine the pain of Maria leaving home. She will always be mine and, with a deepening appreciation of love, I know I, too, will always be the daughter of those who created me. I am my own being, and, at the same time, I belong to them.

**Write a letter of thanksgiving
to one of your creators.**

You have been borne by me
from your birth,
carried from the womb.

—Isaiah 46:3

Nonpossessive Love

Yesterday I thought about my dawning realization, as I move into motherhood, of how much I belong to my mother, father, and God. When I think of my own child, however, I know I cannot live long with the image of her as my possession. She is a gift from God and I need to give her back—to God and to herself. I have the privilege of teaching, caring for, guiding, and loving her. In return she will owe me nothing. But the more perfectly I can love her, the wider I will open the window for her to God's love and her own discovery of herself.

**God, thank you for this precious gift of a child.
Guide my love in purity and not possessiveness.**

> Even when you turn gray
> I will carry you.

—Isaiah 46:4

Touch

I listened to a woman explain to me, the other day, why she doesn't hold her baby any more than necessary. She said that when she returns to work in a few weeks, the childcare providers won't have time to hold all the babies, and, if she spoils him now, he will just be frustrated then.

Something doesn't feel right to me about that logic. I'd rather believe the doctors and books that say it's impossible to spoil a baby. I don't want to train my baby to be deprived, even if that were possible. Besides, I just can't help but hold him every chance I get. If he gets too many hugs, he can reserve the extra ones for days when he doesn't get enough.

Lord, thank you for the well of love
you've given me that keeps spilling out
all over my baby.

Let the little children come to me; do not stop them,
for it is to such as these
that the kingdom of God belongs.
—Mark 10:14

Grandma's Death

On my wedding day, I missed Grandma. She died just before I met John, and I was so sad they would never know each other. I wanted her to know how happy I was with him, and I wanted him to see how wonderful she was.

Now I miss her again. Grandma was on her way to my home within minutes of hearing I was born. She reappeared with the birth of all my brothers and sister, to make apple dumplings and sugar cookies and to play with us while Mother was preoccupied.

I wish she could see my baby now and watch her grow with me. I wish Maria could be blessed by those hands, gnarled by hard work, and hear her hearty laugh. I sure could use one of her fresh apple dumplings about now, too.

**Resolve to be a storyteller,
connecting your baby's generation
to what you know of the past one.**

Precious in the sight of the Lord
is the death of his faithful ones.

—Psalm 116:15

Prayer

Today was Carmen's birthday. I wanted to do something for my special friend, but I knew I had neither the time nor the energy even to call or write to her.

So I lit the big peach candle she gave me for Christmas and burned it all day in the middle of the dining room table. Every time I walked by the burning flame, I thought about Carmen, and I felt warm inside.

I have a feeling Carmen's birthday was special for her, too. Someday I hope to put my love for her back into words, but, for now, I will relax in knowing that my thinking of her today was also a prayer for her.

**Light a candle
for someone you love.**

Arise, shine, for your light has come,
and the glory of the Lord has risen upon you.

—Isaiah 60:1

Marriage

I remember the last vacation we took before the baby was born. My husband looked at my oversized middle and said, "Did you have to bring The Goober (our affectionate attempt to not assign a sex)? I thought this was just going to be the two of us!"

It was a joke. We laughed.

But the "joke" is still here and it's not so funny today. John wants to go out for the evening—just the two of us. But I can't stand thinking about leaving her with someone else if we don't have to. I'd like to be with him alone, but I also want to be with her.

Neither of us is consciously walking away from the other, but this little one sometimes feels like a soft, powerful wedge, settling in between our hearts.

I didn't know this new arrival would force my marriage to change so much.

**Recognize the ways in which you
and your husband differ—
without needing to mesh them all.**

O continue your steadfast love to those who know you.

—Psalm 36:10

Undeserved Love

Today I felt unworthy of love—God's love, John's caresses, and my baby's snuggling. I couldn't even love myself.

Then I watched Jonathan. All his energy is put into receiving, and I love him for it! He does nothing but lie here, needing others to take care of everything for him. He is vulnerable to love (or neglect) without doing anything to earn it. Maybe if I'd focus on being a good receiver, I wouldn't have to analyze my worthiness. Maybe all those who try to love me would have an easier job doing it then, too. If I weren't spending time weighing my worthiness, I might have more time left to love.

Know that by definition,
you,
a child of God, are worthy of love.

You shall love your neighbor
as yourself.

—Matthew 19:19

A Challenging Gift

During the ten years I worked in prisons and centers for juvenile delinquents, I wondered why anyone would want to have children. They are heartbreakers. They make choices contrary to the wisdom of their elders. They complicate life.

Now, one look at the child lying peacefully in the crib beside me gives me the answer. Yes, she will likely break my heart. She won't choose as I have. She will definitely complicate my life.

I receive her life as a gift, however, and my role as a challenge. I stand in awe of her and in need of God's assistance like never before.

God, help me always see my child as a gift
rather than a possession to be controlled.

In your book were written all the days
that were formed for me,
when none of them as yet existed.
—Psalm 139:16

Personhood of Baby

"I'm going stir-crazy! I haven't had anyone to see or talk to all day," I complained when my husband called from work.

"What happened to the other person who was with you when I left this morning?" he asked. After I got done blaming him for being insensitive, I realized that I do need to start thinking of this tiny bundle as the person she is, no matter where she is on the scale of relational skills.

I find myself being eager for her to respond to me, to move, to talk, to anticipate with me, and to do lunch together. Unless I recognize her personhood right now, however, it may be difficult to see it later.

She won't meet all the needs that an adult friend can, but that's not her job. She is a person, though, and one with whom I have a relationship. I don't feel quite so alone anymore.

God, I'm grateful that you continue to relate to me even though I must seem

**as far below your relational skill level
as my baby sometimes seems to me.**

What are human beings that you are mindful of them . . . ?
Yet you have made them a little lower than God, and
crowned them with glory and honor.

—Psalm 8:4, 5

Circle of Love

This is like a second honeymoon! When we first got married, I remember being awestruck by receiving so many gifts with no need to reciprocate. No one disputed our need for time alone. We couldn't be together enough.

We are again flooded with gifts and excused from responsibilities. As the rest of the world moves on, we sit here gazing into each other's eyes, basking in our love and the creation of our new family, reveling in every movement and sound that comes from the most recent addition to our circle of love.

**Relish all the gifts
that welcome you to motherhood.**

She is free and she is our mother.
—Galatians 4:26

Brand-New Life

It's the same old thing, but it's brand new. It's happened over and over, but this is the first time it's ever happened. Children have been born every day since the beginning of time, but this is the first one born to me in my time.

It's not a routine thing that I just did by giving birth. It's not normal to suddenly be sharing our home with a baby. There is nothing ordinary about this complete change of schedule. My way of thinking about space, God, myself, and love is forever changed.

It's my brand-new life and I love it.

**Thank you, God,
for the freshness you give to me
in this ageless event.**

He put a new song in my mouth.

—Psalm 40:3

Bliss

I have always loved words. The more different words I can find to say the same thing, the better.

But my vocabulary has been greatly reduced lately. I've noticed that I say things like, "You're so precious," and "I love you," and "You're so beautiful," over and over. I'm not offering much variety. It's not creative language. It's just the bliss of motherhood, plain and simple.

**Force yourself to think
of one new adjective
to use for your baby today!**

There is no speech, nor are there words.

—Psalm 19:3

Worry

I worry about so many things. Is my baby getting enough to eat? Is he getting too much? Am I building up fat cells so he will have to be on a diet the rest of his life? Will he get sick if I let him play with kids with runny noses? Will he get his social needs met if he doesn't go to day care? What if he stops breathing?

Sometimes I act like I, alone, am responsible for his whole life.

Give thanks for all the things that are well with your baby and all the help you have in child-rearing.

Do not worry about anything, but in everything by prayer and supplication, with thanksgiving, let your requests be made known to God.

—Philippians 4:6

Exhaustion

This past weekend I saw an old friend at a wedding. Knowing she had just had a baby the month before, I asked about her energy supply.

"Oh, I have all of it back!" she said happily.

"Quit lying to me," I laughed. "I know when your baby was born!" Thirty minutes later, I saw her sitting listless in a corner at the reception. This exhaustion, however, was not the part of motherhood she willingly shared or talked about.

Maybe that's why I feel so alone in my exhaustion. I only see other new mothers when they have the energy to get out of the house. They only call me when they feel good enough to tell me how good they feel.

I, too, like to tell people I'm doing fine. But that doesn't comfort anyone, especially when it's not true most of the time!

Be honest with another mother.
You may hear the relief of returned honesty
to keep you company.

Be gracious to me, O Lord,
for to you do I cry all day long.

—Psalm 86.3

Children of God

It's easy to see, when I look at my tiny baby, that he is created in beauty by God—it's obvious that only God could be in charge of calling him forth, complete in these few pounds, with all the organs and brain cells he needs to grow into a man. I can believe, without hesitation, that God will continue to watch over his soul and call forth what has already begun for the rest of his life.

As I can easily see God loving and continuing to call my son, I know God's love and calling to be for me as well. It has already begun and will go on for the rest of my life.

Thank you, God,
for parenting both of us at the same time.

The Lord called me before I was born,
while I was in my mother's womb he named me.
—Isaiah 49:1

A Girl

I wasn't aware of having a preference for a boy or a girl, but the minute I knew my baby was a girl, my heart jumped in joy. Not only was this my own flesh and blood, but we would also share the agony and wonder of being female.

That same fact has since put fear into my heart as well. Every time I hear about a little girl being raped or I learn the statistics that say a high percentage of all females will be molested at some point in their lives, I cringe. I want to cling to her and never let her out of my sight.

Studies done of children who have been molested say that it is not always preventable, but the long-lasting effect on the child is determined by whether or not the child has an adult who listens to her and believes her. Secrecy is the most damaging element.

**God,
help me to learn how to listen
to my daughter.**

See, we are your bone and flesh.
—I Chronicles 11:1

Shoulds

"Get rid of the 'shoulds' in your life." That sounded like strange advice from my friend, but the more I think about it, the more it makes sense. I live too much according to "shoulds," which tend to oppress rather than give life. Should statements include:

Good Mothers

should stay at home with their children.

should use cloth diapers.

should never show their anger.

should always do creative activities with their children and keep a clean house and serve balanced meals and entertain guests and make fresh cookies every week . . .

I don't know who sends all those "should" messages, but I do have a choice about whether or not I let them control me. If I monitor my own family's needs, including my own, and meet them as well as I can, I won't have to pay attention to the outside "shoulds." I may still make the same choices as the "shoulds" dictate, but if it's because I want to, I live out those choices in freedom instead of bondage.

God, help me separate your voice from the others that clamor for my attention.

Where the Spirit of the Lord is, there is freedom.

—II Corinthians 3:17

Isolation

It is so strange to be home in the middle of the day. I wonder what other people are doing. I call a friend, but her answering machine clicks on. I remember that it's Tuesday. Of course, she's at work.

I switch on the TV—only soap operas. I look out the window and notice an unusual emptiness. The ears are all at work, too. I dress my baby and go shopping. Everyone moves like they have somewhere to go. They probably do. We go for a long walk. It feels odd to go without a return deadline.

I have all the time I used to long for. Now I feel cut off from the rest of the world—the world I've known for so many years. I need to recreate my whole way of thinking about life for this time at home with my baby! People tell me this time will go quickly, but today I believe it will last forever.

God, help me endure my blessings.

"I am not alone because the Father is with me."
—John 16:32

Awareness Heightened

When I was ten years old, I slept through a storm that blew our family's tent down on us. My sister and I often wakened on the opposite side of the bed from where we fell asleep, without remembering who rolled over whom.

I still sleep through thunder, dogs barking, and alarm clocks. Suddenly, however, I'm waking up several times a night to a new sound in our house—the cry of our baby! I wake up if his breathing is labored. I wake up if it's been too long since I heard him, and I walk over to make sure he's still alive.

I used to call and call when I needed God. I thought I wasn't being heard!

**God, thank you for showing yourself to me
through this ten-pound example.**

The Lord is near to all who call on him . . .
he also hears their cry and saves them.
—Psalm 145:18, 19

Gentleness

I never knew I had so much gentleness in me! The nurses handled my baby like a football, but I don't find any roughness within myself. I feel a little silly kissing my sleeping baby, but I can't seem to help it! I pat him, rocking and singing, long after he needs it to fall asleep. His soft skin, tiny fingers, and cuddly body, sinking into mine, melt my hurried, calculated affection.

Gentleness and I are one. It might sound strange to someone else, but it doesn't to me now that I'm a mother.

**God,
this gentleness must be of you
because I certainly haven't had to work at it.
Thank you.**

Let your gentleness be known to everyone.
—Philippians 4:5

Misunderstood

If having a baby is such a common ordinary thing to do, why do I feel so alone? Why do I feel like no one can possibly understand what I'm going through? Did all those other mothers in the rooms down the hall from me in the hospital, who looked so delighted to have given birth and so patient as they changed their first diapers, go home and cry, too, because they were suddenly alone with their responsibilities?

If anyone is able to understand me right now, she's probably too busy or tired to let me know! I never feel like I have the time and energy to pick up the phone, anyway.

I hope the reason people don't talk about these feelings is because they're over so quickly and then forgotten. Today motherhood feels lonely with no end in sight.

**Thank you, God, for listening
and understanding, even when I don't.**

Then they cried to the Lord in their trouble,
and he saved them from their distress.

—Psalm 107:19

Exhausted

Some days I'm too tired to wash, too tired to get dressed, too tired to make something to eat, and too tired to put things away. I can get by with not doing those things for a short while, but eventually I make myself do them.

Some days I'm too tired to relate to my husband, too tired to be a friend, and too tired to think about God. I've worried that I'm losing my personality, my etiquette, my responsibility, and my spirituality.

Then I feel God smile and say, "It's all still here within you. You may not recognize it through all your many changes. Be patient with yourself."

**God,
whoever and wherever you are,
thank you.**

Charm is deceitful and beauty is vain,
but a woman who fears the Lord is to be praised.
—Proverbs 31:30

Misjudging

Will I ever learn how to judge my time and energy correctly? I know in my head that I can't do as much as before I had a baby, but I still never seem to reduce my to-do list enough.

I think I'm doing well when I plan to make two phone calls after supper is cleaned up, instead of five, and write a few short notes after the baby's in bed, instead of a long letter.

But at midnight I wake up on the couch with the baby in my arms. Too tired to mind the stack of dirty dishes, and vowing to be in touch with my friends tomorrow, I drop off to sleep again, baby still in my arms. Sometimes we make it to our own beds. Sometimes not.

Come to think of it, I always have made longer lists than I can do. This is just one weakness motherhood has accented.

Don't do today what can be put off until tomorrow.

And the peace of God, which surpasses all understanding, will guard your hearts and your minds in Christ Jesus.

—Philippians 4:7

Mother's Boundaries

Ever since high school, I have consciously worked at finding the balance between loving others and loving myself. This new relationship with a baby, however, is a more intense responsibility than I could ever have imagined, pre-motherhood! The temptation is to give her everything I have—all my energy, all my love, all my time. I know that doing that would eventually smother her beyond her wishes and shrivel me dry at the same time.

Now, while my child will take everything I have to offer, I want to stay aware of how to meet my needs, too. Only as I am filled can I pour out again. I not only want my child to grow up happy, I want her to call me happy.

**What makes you
a happy woman?**

Her children rise up and call her happy.
—Proverbs 31:28

Tension

I'm having a hard time knowing how to make parenting decisions *with* my husband, when he's unavailable for a lot of the daily judgment calls. I can't telephone him at work every time I have a question about childcare or how to feed the baby or a purchase that seems necessary.

Maybe what's hardest is knowing that no matter how equal we intend our parenting to be, I am primarily responsible for taking care of the baby now. I want to do that, but in a way that doesn't exclude his involvement when he does have the time and energy to give it.

**Admitting where the tension lies
can be a large part of the solution.**

Teach me good judgment and knowledge.
—Psalm 119:66

Change

Help! What's happening? I'm growing more and more incompetent. My physical powers are caving in on me. It's not time for a midlife crisis yet!

While I feel like I'm coming apart, my head keeps trying to calm me. "Slow down. Take charge of your life." The truth is I feel less in control than ever! I've relinquished some of that control (a lot of it many days!) to this new member of the family. While I'm busy caring for her, I reach the edge of my limits without noticing. Suddenly I feel myself going over it in exhaustion.

It might help if I could admit and remember that the edge is a little closer right now. It won't be this way forever.

**Go ahead
and loosen your grip.**

All things are wearisome,
more than one can express.

—Ecclesiastes 1:8

Mother's Illness

Here comes another new experience for which I was not prepared! I feel awful today—the stuffy-nose, sore-eyes, thick-neck, heavy-head kind of awful. It's the kind of awful that I have learned exactly how to heal over the years. I go to bed for a couple of days and sleep it off.

That strategy doesn't fit so well anymore. How do mothers get well while life proceeds normally for the youngest member of the household? She is obviously not going to get dressed, eat, and play by herself!

This job doesn't have sick leave! There must be another strategy for healing mothers.

O God,
give me strength and patience
to live one moment at a time.

Be gracious to me, O Lord,
for I am languishing.

—Psalm 6:2

Feeling Inadequate

I was so embarrassed. They hadn't told me they were coming. One moment I was blissfully playing with my baby and the next I was painfully aware of the sink full of dirty dishes, the smell of dirty diapers oozing from the bedroom, my unbathed child, and my own shirt ripe with the stench of sour milk.

It wasn't until after they left that I realized I had robbed myself of the joy of sharing her, so preoccupied had I been with trying to look like the model mom. Why do I do that?

Mary certainly didn't have ideal conditions to let the world meet Jesus. Yet the angels proclaimed his birth, as if his meager layette were the way to present royalty. We celebrate the manger in the same way every Christmas—as if there couldn't have been a more romantic way to give birth. I wonder if Mary was embarrassed when the shepherds showed up.

**God help me live with this child
in the spirit of Christ's birth, humble**

**and simple, without needing
the approval of the masses.**

You will find a child wrapped in hands of cloth
and lying in a manger.

—Luke 2:12

Music

I've been told that babies love to hear the voices of their parents singing to them, no matter how off-key or crackly the sound. I was sure my child would rather listen to the lullaby tapes I bought as a backup.

Amazingly enough, she fits the norm! She seems to be soothed by my singing, so I'm learning to sing without worrying about perfection. It's been fun to resurrect songs from deep in my memory and relive the childhood comfort of my parents singing to me. It's become a time of worship as I imagine God holding both of us as we all rock and sing together!

**Fill your day
with music.**

I will praise the Lord as long as I live;
I will sing praises to my God all my life long.
—Psalm 146:2

Postpartum Depression

I cried myself to sleep again last night. I kept telling myself to snap out of it, but I lacked the gusto to listen. I know that, contrary to many others in the world, I have a safe home to live in, friends and relatives who love me, and food for my family. But tears don't make intellectual comparisons, and they kept coming.

A phone call triggered them. A phone call from someone who was oblivious to my child crying in my arms, who ignored my weariness and talked on and on about problems I'd already listened to three times. I didn't even have enough energy to assert myself.

I finally hung up, irrationally and completely furious. Then I allowed myself to be tired and miserable and fell asleep. Some days are just like that—especially by the end.

Let your tears be to God,
who understands and loves you in the midst of them.

My tears have been my food day and night.

—Psalm 42:3

Nurturing

I'm watching myself, like in a dream, amazed at all the nurturing skills I see coming so naturally from myself. Pre-motherhood, I watched mothers kiss their babies over and over and I knew I could never be that gushy. I saw their patience with screaming babies and decided I'd rather lock them in a closet than listen to that!

I didn't decide to change, but I know now that I have. Kissing and hugging my baby seem more like reflexes than decisions. Cries are simply her language.

I am thankful to my hormones for my increased nurturing skills. And I am thankful to my Creator for the miracle of hormones that continually prepare me for the next step and help me understand, to a greater extent, how much I am loved.

**Your increased nurturing skills
may not count professionally, but have eternal value.**

As a mother comforts her child, so I will comfort you.

—Isaiah 66:13

Homebody

I find evidence of God's caring about little things in the fact that Maria was born on a Friday night. I've always felt driven to do something out of the ordinary on Friday night. I don't mind staying home any other night of the week, but find me home doing nothing special on a Friday evening and you'll be looking at a sad woman!

I remember those feelings now, two months after her birth, as if they belonged to someone else. That was the last Friday night I "went out." Strangely enough, caring for a baby on Friday nights is filling my need for action. Call me boring. Call me a party pooper. I call myself full of joy!

**Make no apologies
for the changes
you are enjoying.**

Let the faithful exult in glory:
let them sing for joy on their couches.

—Psalm 149:5

Illness

My whole body aches. I don't know if I'm catching my baby's cold or if I'm just sore from being tense. I can't sleep at night because I keep hearing her labored breathing. And if I don't hear it, I jump up to make sure she's still alive!

All day I wonder whether or not I should give her medicine. Is she in pain or just tired? Is it best to let her fight it on her own? Is she bad enough to take to the doctor?

It's so hard to make judgments for this tiny bundle. I wish she could tell me what hurts. They say mothers just know what to do, but sometimes I just don't!

Thank goodness I'm not the first one to go through this. I think I'll go call a friend.

**Thank God for the resources you have
to help you handle your precious charge.**

O God,
please heal her.

—Numbers 12:13

Fourth Trimester

For nine months I put up with being tired and nauseated. I laughed with my friends who couldn't help noticing my clumsiness and forgetfulness. I was unusually disorganized and blamed it on my pregnancy. I had inner work to do, to prepare for my baby, that took precedence over the outside world.

I expected to snap out of those inconveniences once the baby arrived, though, and I haven't. I'm still tired and forgetful, and I feel pressure to be what others expect of me, to be normal again. Then a friend said to me, "Just call this your fourth trimester." Now that's the kind of friend I'm willing to have influence me!

**Give yourself a break from expectations:
others' and your own.**

Come to me,
all you who are weary . . .
and I will give you rest.
—Matthew 11:28

Prayer

My mother casually remarked the other day that she figures it's the job of women her age to pray for women in my life-stage. She said new mothers don't have time to do it.

How did she know? I would have never admitted to her that I hardly ever pray anymore! But she said it as if it's a well-known fact and she didn't expect a response. How refreshing that the breach in my prayers doesn't have to be my guilt-laden secret!

I miss the early morning quiet time I had with God, pre-baby. After being up two or three times during the night, though, sleep seems more important. Mother's offhand comment gives me permission to enjoy sleeping and my child.

**Thank you, Lord, for my mother,
and all the mother figures in the world who pray
for those of us just being added to their numbers.**

I thank my God every time I remember you.
—Philippians 1:3

God as Baby

"God's love came to us as a tiny baby." How many Christmas stories have I heard in which that truth was reported? Too many, apparently, because I was never amazed by it. Never, that is, until I heard it while holding my own tiny one.

Maybe it wasn't possible to let that vulnerable, dependent, weak form of God fill me with wonder until I cared for a child of God myself. When I feel too young, in my thirties, to be responsible for a child, I am bewildered that God entrusted a girl of fourteen or fifteen to carry, nurture, and help shape the life of Jesus.

I can't imagine any greater form of trust in people, nor any more profound way of learning what it is to be human. God, alone, would choose such an act!

**Treat your child, today,
as if he or she were the Christ child.**

The child to be born will be holy;
he will be called the Son of God.

—Luke 1:35

Changing Lifestyle

Life seems to have moved into Act II since the moment Maria was born. This part is not as goal-oriented as Act I. My adjustment and acceptance of this must be a gift from God, because I would not have changed this much on my own. I'm discovering it to be extremely important, however, for my current survival.

Where I once felt interrupted by a ringing phone, another adult's voice is now a welcome change. Where unexpected visitors were chaos in my order, they now join with me in what I'm already doing—holding my baby. Instead of scheduling walks, I go when the urge hits. I even take naps in the middle of the day!

Most amazing is that the world seems to be going on just fine, even without all my contributions! That doesn't seem quite right, but I'll worry about that another day.

Even God rested after creating humanity.

. . . and [God] rested on the seventh day
from all the work that he had done.
—Genesis 2:2

First Night Out

I couldn't believe I was the first to leave the party. This baby has made me a different woman! Tonight was the first time I left my husband alone to feed Maria and put her to bed.

I rushed home and through the door, expecting chaos. What met me was peace! All evening I had imagined Maria crying inconsolably for me, and here she was, sleeping! The house was clean and the dishes done.

Relief mixed strangely with annoyance. How dare they get along so easily without me? I guess I can relax a little and not assume I'm running the show by myself.

**If you feel too responsible,
give up some of it
and see who picks up the pieces.**

Surely goodness and mercy
shall follow me all the days of my life.

—Psalm 23:6

Animals

I never thought to worry about Tipper being jealous of the baby. It makes sense, though, since he gets less attention now.

But true to a dog's nature, he doesn't hold a grudge. He still takes whatever love we have left for him, whenever we have time to give it. He even sniffs the baby in a caring, curious sort of way.

His dog noises seem to be a natural part of Maria's world already. He barks in the room where she's sleeping without awakening her. She must remember the sound from *in utero*!

Maybe we can all learn to incorporate his loving, forgiving nature into our lives as well!

**Help us learn,
O God, even from our dog!**

But ask the animals,
and they will teach you.

—Job 12:7

Resentment

I wanted this baby for a long time, so I feel a little guilty saying it, but sometimes I resent her presence. Loving her is more a decision than a feeling when she wakes me up at night, doesn't go to sleep when I want her to, and spits up all over me at a party.

How can such a tiny baby demand so much? I have no time to myself anymore. Every conversation I start gets interrupted. I can't even have one nice quiet dinner with my husband. She's controlling my time, my relationships, my emotions. No textbook prepared me for this!

**God, help me give of myself to this child,
rather than think of her as taking from me.**

And babes shall rule over them.

—Isaiah 3:4

Resentment Reversed

Yesterday, I was nearly overwhelmed with resentment. Today the sun is shining warmly on me as I sit by the window after a night of unusually good sleep. What a difference those simple gifts can make in my attitude! Today I am grateful for the recent changes in my life.

No one has ever needed me like this baby needs me. She depends on me for everything, much longer than other animals depend on their mothers.

I feel special when she sees me and stops crying. I feel grateful that I have food to give her when she cries with hunger, clothes to put on her when she's cold, and a bed in which to lay her when she's tired. Not all mothers have all those resources when their babies cry. With that knowledge, I can put up with some of the inconveniences.

**Thank you, God,
for allowing me to love and care for this child of yours.**

[John] will go before him,
to turn the hearts of parents to their children.
—Luke 1:17

Blessing

After a special service of dedicating our baby and ourselves to God, the pastor approached us. He put his hand on our son's head, looked into his eyes, and quietly spoke his name.

That's all he said. That's all he needed to say. That was his whole prayer. In that instant, I knew how marvelous it must have been for mothers to watch Jesus touch their infants. I knew our son was being blessed by Jesus—through this man's hand.

**Bless your child today
with your touch.**

People were bringing
even infants to [Jesus]
that he might touch them.

—Luke 18:15

One Day at a Time

It's funny how fast motherhood hit. One day I was a relatively free woman, and the next I was overloaded with responsibility for another soul. Instantly, the role of mother was stamped on my identity, and I will carry it for the rest of my days. Even if I become Grandma someday, I will still be a mother as well.

It's a bit overwhelming to think about all motherhood will mean. I guess no one else expects me to know everything instantly, so I may as well give up expecting it, too.

I will grow and learn with my child. I'd do well to adopt the motto of many self-help groups: "One day at a time."

**Tape "One Day at a Time"
to your bathroom mirror.**

Every day I will bless you,
and praise your name, forever and ever.

—Psalm 145:2

Forgive

On our evening walks, John and I share an old joke—we can always tell which one of us has had the worst day by who yells at the dog the most.

These days we barely ever have our evening walks. On top of that, it seems like I'm always the one who's had the worst day without the luxury of a dog to yell at. No, I don't take it out on the baby (thank God). I just get irritated with everything John does!

It's hard to distinguish between what he does that's really offensive and when I'm reacting out of my tiredness. I haven't really tried to tell. I've just been yelling at him about everything!

**God, renew a tender heart within me
instead of letting me lash out at the one I most love.**

Be kind to one another, tenderhearted,
forgiving one another,
as God in Christ has forgiven you.
—Ephesians 4:32

Transience

The transient nature of my world hit me hard today. One of my closest friends told me they are planning to move. This is the friend whose first baby arrived five weeks before mine; the one with whom I've found it easiest to share the ups and downs of this new life of motherhood.

Since my baby was born, I've thought more about the need to offer her stability than I've ever thought about needing it for myself. Now I realize that even if I stay in the same place, I have no guarantee of stability!

Sometimes I have the fleeting illusion of having control of my life. Today I see again how little control I have. The only sure thing is that my world will continue to change.

**God, thank you for the constancy
of your love and companionship.**

Neither death, nor life, nor angels, nor rulers, nor things present, nor things to come, nor powers, nor height, nor depth, nor anything else in all creation will be able to separate us from the love of God in Christ Jesus our Lord.
—Romans 8:38, 39

Solitude

A friend confided to me this morning that she's nervous about going on a guided tour to Europe. She isn't sure she can be with twenty other people for three solid weeks and remain the affable person she wants to be. I encouraged her to find as much time alone as she needs, even if the rest of the group doesn't always understand. She thanked me for permission to meet her own needs.

After she left, I thought about how I could certainly use someone to give me the same kind of permission. I didn't think it sounded selfish to encourage my friend to do it, but that's what I fear when I think about salvaging some time alone for myself. As a new mother I need even more solitude than I used to, to remain the decent person I want to be.

**Receive the permission,
yes, the invitation from God, to be still.**

Be still,
and know that I am God!

—Psalm 46:10

Priorities

I'm finally learning to control my impulse to respond to anyone and everyone who calls. After I stumbled to the phone four times during one feeding, with my tired baby jiggled awake each time, I realized that I don't *have* to answer the phone just because it's ringing. After being awakened from a precious nap by yet another salesman, I began peeking out the window before opening the door.

It took a tiny baby to help me realize that my time is a gift I give by my choice, rather than by others' demands. I love this baby too much to have her disturbed unduly, and I can learn to love myself that much, too!

**Check your responses today
for whether or not
they are your conscious choices.**

You, O Lord,
are a shield around me, my glory,
and the one who lifts up my head.

—Psalm 3:3

Loneliness

All week I have become increasingly aware of being lonely. I wanted to have friends over, but I know John comes home, weary from working with people all day. He often wants to relax in his own home, around his own family for the evening. Besides, I don't want him to think I'm not enjoying being with the baby.

But tonight, on the verge of exploding, I finally told him how lonely I've been. He held me and told me how much he loves me. In his understanding, my hurt began to heal. I thought I was protecting him from the ups and downs of my feelings, but what I was really doing was depriving myself of his love.

**Be vulnerable
and open yourself to love.**

As God's chosen ones,
holy, beloved, clothe yourselves
with compassion, kindness, humility,
meekness, and patience.

—Colossians 3:12

Watching Television

As I was watching one of my favorite shows tonight, it suddenly looked different to me. When my son is old enough to comprehend the words I'm hearing, I don't know if I want him to listen to this! Even before that, he will see the pictures. Will he assume these are the actions I condone? To enjoy the humor, I've overlooked some details that could be destructive to a growing, learning child who absorbs a high percentage of what he sees and hears.

This baby is changing how I see my whole world! Maybe the changes could lead to a more wholesome life for me as well.

**Do your television practices need to change—
at least when your child is awake?**

Let each of you look
not to your own interests,
but to the interests of others.

—Philippians 2:4

Responsibility

I'm amazed, sometimes, at the wisdom that is woven into children's stories. I read a book this week to a four-year-old about children growing up on a planet that was so tiny it couldn't hold them down. Earth, on the other hand, was big enough to hold people down. In fact, it pulled down so hard that the children had to exercise their muscles in preparation for a trip to earth where they would need to pick up their feet to walk or run.

I found myself in that story. By adding the responsibility of a baby to my life, I feel myself pulled down more easily. I try to figure out the future, or I worry about bills. Maybe if I'd dwell, instead, on how much bigger my world has become because of this new life, I'd be more eager to stretch myself into the possibilities, instead of letting my thinking muscles get pulled down.

**Lord, show me the spiritual exercises
that will help me walk more easily
in this new responsibility.**

Praise your God, O Zion!
For he strengthens the bars of your gates;
he blesses your children within you.
—Psalm 147:13

Balancing Needs

Yesterday I was thinking about the importance of putting my child's needs before my own. Today I realize that if I do that 100 percent, my child will lose who I really am and so will I. If I always look out for others, I'll lose the flame within me, and, consequently, my vision, my creativity, my spiritual self.

If I lose myself, I'll have nothing left to give. If I look inside to meet my own needs, I will have increased life, energy, and love to give.

Lord,
help me find a good balance
between meeting my needs
and meeting the needs of my child.

[Jesus] would withdraw to deserted
places and pray.

—Luke 5:16

Anger

Today I remember quite clearly why I resisted the parenting stage for so long. I have to give up two more things that have been part of me for as long as I can remember. For the first time in my life, I didn't meet a writing deadline. I had planned to finish the assignment with all those hours a sleeping newborn provides. I haven't even turned on the computer.

Last night at chorus practice, the one outlet I was determined to keep, I was miserably exhausted. I couldn't concentrate. The notes on my score began to blur. I can't stay up that late anymore.

I hate giving up so much.

God,
please receive my anger
so it doesn't make its way to my baby.

With your faithful help,
rescue me from sinking in the mire.
—Psalm 69:13, 14

Double Shift

One of my friends explained her exhaustion this week by telling me how many double shifts she's done at work in the past ten days. All of a sudden I understood my own utter weariness.

On the days I go to work I no longer come home and relax. I jump into the next shift. Depending on what the night is like, sometimes I'm on call for the third shift as well. On the days I'm home all day, I don't get the satisfaction of "punching out" after eight hours. Breaks are not dependable, there's no lunch break, and the workload is no respecter of energy levels. Pacing myself has to be incorporated into this new job description that I'm still writing.

Give yourself credit
for all the double shifts you do.

May the Lord give you increase,
both you and your children.
—Psalm 115:14

Lack of Production

When I was pregnant, my life felt like the image I have of a newspaper office—full of flurry and busyness, meeting deadlines in the nick of time, never getting enough sleep. Things that I didn't have to do before the baby was born, I put on a separate pile, to be done when the baby was sleeping.

Surprise! Three months later the pile is still there. The flurry did let up for a time, but so did my energy. No one could have told me how little I would accomplish after giving birth. I can't explain it adequately to anyone else either. It's just one of those facts you have to be a mother to learn, and you can't be a mother without learning it!

**God,
continue to help me learn
the facts of life.**

God is
our refuge and strength.

—Psalm 46:1

Sleep

I hate it when I go back to bed at night after being up with the baby, and I can't sleep. I'm exhausted, and I know I won't be able to function well tomorrow if I don't get my sleep; then I get so upset about not being able to sleep that I'm more awake than ever. I'm in a total, tired tizzy!

So I imagine I'm lying on the beach. I let the warmth of the sun soak into my skin. I let the water flow over me: first my feet, then up to my neck. The sand slowly pulls out from under me as the water recedes. Magically, I breathe in the water as it returns and washes gently over my whole body. I sink deeper and deeper into the sand and . . . that's all I usually remember!

**Practice a prayer of relaxation
to use the next time you experience insomnia.**

My mouth praises you with joyful lips
when I think of you on my bed,
and meditate on you in the watches of the night.
—Psalm 63:5, 6

Mystery Child

I was watching a group of children playing in the park today, wondering what my baby will be like when she's that old. Will she like the slide or the swings better? Will she be a climber? What will her laugh sound like? Will she talk a lot, like me, or keep her thoughts largely within, like her dad, or be some combination of the two of us? Will she like to sing or work in the garden or bake or teach or write poetry?

I wonder if I'll be able to let her make her own decisions. I guess that's the only part I can determine. I have carried, birthed, and nurtured this child more closely than I have lived with any other person. To a large extent, however, she remains a mystery and, to some extent, will always be a mystery.

**God, help me to accept the choices
of this blossoming person.**

Even before a word is on my tongue,
O Lord, you know it completely.
—Psalm 139:4

Answered Prayer

I never really liked children. I turned down babysitting jobs as a teenager and thought babies were universally ugly when I took the time to look at them at all. Most of my friends were in the single or married-without-children category.

When my biological clock forced me into a decision, however, I determined to try this parenting thing everyone else seemed to think was so wonderful. The longer it took me to get pregnant, the more I was consumed by a growing desire to be a mother. My prayers of "Should I . . . ?" became cries of "Please, God . . ."

When the pregnancy test came back positive, however, fear set in again. What if I didn't like my own child? What if The Goober was ugly?

What a waste of energy! I continue to marvel at God's overwhelming answer to my request to be filled with love for my baby.

**Let God add another puff of love
to the balloon in your heart.**

For this child I prayed,
and the Lord has granted me the petition
that I made.

—I Samuel 1:27

Separation Anxiety

A friend offered to stay with my baby the other day so I could take a break. I had dreamed of going for a walk alone or just sitting and thinking without needing to listen for his waking cry.

It was a splendid offer and a wonderful thought, but I couldn't seem to relax. I spent the whole time worrying about the baby. Was he okay? Did I remember to tell her everything? Was he crying for me to come back?

When I returned from the ordeal, he greeted me with a smiling face. I had been the only one with separation anxiety!

**You may as well start learning right now
how to let go of your child!**

Peace be with you.

—Luke 24:36

Valuing My Work

"What did you do today?"

I used to love to be asked that question. I took pride in my busyness and productivity. Now it's a question I hate. What I do now can't be calculated like most people measure tasks. I'm busy all day, but I don't have much tangible evidence to remind me of what I did, much less to recount to someone else.

I was a mother today. I loved today, not always perfectly, but I did love. I didn't earn any money today, but I did contribute to the good of the world. I was a mother.

**Thank you, God,
for giving me so valuable a job.**

Do your best to present yourself to God
as one approved by him,
a worker who has no need to be ashamed.

—II Timothy 2:15

Owned or Loaned?

Some days I nearly burst with joy when I think about this newly acquired possession I have in the baby I hold. I'm proud to show her to friends and strangers alike and let everyone know she belongs to me!

Other days I am humbled to think of her as the gift she is, on loan from her Maker. I've been invited to help her learn and to be taught by her as well. I won't care for my child perfectly, but with the help of the One who created this baby and me, I will be a good mother.

**Thinking of my baby as a gift on loan
helps me cherish our moments together
more than ever!**

The earth is the Lord's
and all that is in it,
the world,
and those who live in it.

—Psalm 24:1

Respect

Before I was a parent, I knew how to be the best parent
. . . of course. I most admired the ones who main-
tained the same lifestyle with their babies as they had lived
before. They went on all the same camping trips and bike
rides. No baby was going to get in the way of their com-
mittee work, late nights out, or early morning fishing trips.
The baby could go along and adjust to their schedules.

That once looked appealing. Now that the idea of my
baby has turned into a real person, however, I can't do it. If
I'm going to respect him as a member of the family, I have
to start now, by letting him have a routine he can learn to
count on. He won't always get what he wants, but I can't
always get what I want either.

**Be attentive to the rhythms
of your child.**

A little child
shall lead them.

—Isaiah 11:6

Development

The last time Anne and I talked about our babies, who are almost the same age, she said hers was finally sleeping through the night. Now I know all babies learn different things at different rates, and mine isn't developmentally delayed just because she only sleeps six hours at one stretch, but I still couldn't help wishing she would be keeping up with her peer at least on this one. Have I been doing something wrong? How can I help her catch up?

Then today Anne mentioned getting up at 5 a.m. with her baby. I said I thought she was sleeping all night. Anne said, "Yeah, she is. She sleeps from eleven to five every night."

I guess it's all in the definition. I was waiting for "all night" to be 8 p.m. to 8 a.m. That will teach me to compare . . . maybe.

God, help me to quit comparing babies.
Help me to focus, instead,
on the miracle of my own baby's development.

My frame was not hidden from you
when I was being made in secret,
intricately woven in the depths of the earth.
—Psalm 139:15

Current Creation

If I didn't know God before, I'm sure I would have begun to believe the moment I first saw this baby. Sure I did my part. I lived through the nausea and colds with no medicine. Well, I didn't take much, anyway. I ate healthily—most of the time. I tried to reduce my stress and sometimes it worked.

There's still a huge part of her development, however, with which I had nothing to do. I just watched and felt God creating in my body. I continue to watch in amazement and thanksgiving as her little fingers learn to develop, her immunities fight off intruders, her throat utters new sounds. What a gift! What a God!

**At each birth of a child,
God, also,
is born anew.**

Fools say in their hearts,
"There is no God."

—Psalm 53:1

Freedom

Last night I just had to get out of the house. Jonathan had been cranky for two days, and even though I knew there was likely a good reason—teething, coming down with a cold, or the heat—I had run out of patience. I called a friend and begged her to go out with me. I didn't care what we did.

As I joyfully dashed out the door, my husband asked when I'd be back. I assured him I'd be gone until the baby was in bed for the night and I'd peek through the porch window and wait for that moment if I had to.

Freedom never felt sweeter. Today I'm ready to be a mother again.

**Thank you, God,
for the spurts of freedom
that revive my commitment to mothering.**

My heart is glad, and my soul rejoices;
my body also rests secure.

—Psalm 16:9

Barrenness

One of my friends came over for supper last night to tell us the doctors confirmed that she'll never be able to have children. The precipitating event made the news even worse. It was because of the damage done to her when she was sexually abused as a child.

I didn't know what to say. I wanted to share my baby and hide her at the same time. My perfect child seemed a glaring imitation of her lost hope. A useless guilt clutched at my stomach that felt saddened to sickness.

I finally realized, however, that losing my joy would not lessen her pain. She just needed me to be with her, to share it, baby and all.

**Lord,
help me to balance the joy of my child
with the pain of her childlessness.**

A time to weep,
and a time to laugh.

—Ecclesiastes 3:4

Living in the Present

Some days I live in the past. I get embarrassed all over again about the stupid things I've done. Or I smile again with the wonderful memories.

Some days I live in the future. Those days I occasionally anticipate a planned event, but I usually worry about what might happen.

The most magical of days, though, are the ones when I live in the present. I suddenly have more time to really look at my baby, really love my husband, and really appreciate my home and the world outside my windows. With my additional time and attention, my gratefulness also swells until I know that I am one rich woman!

Live the entire day in the present.

Whatever is true, whatever is honorable,
whatever is just, whatever is pure, whatever is pleasing,
whatever is commendable, if there is any excellence
and if there is anything worthy of praise,
think about these things.

—Philippians 4:8

Miraculous

I heard a friend say that he appreciates his second child even more than his first. He thinks it's because they were told during the pregnancy that the second child may have Down's syndrome. After months of worrying, he was incredibly relieved to be delivered a healthy boy. Now, he said, he thanks God every day, for the miraculously normal growth of his son.

Life contains a joyful spirit when I see normal things as the miracle they are. My child, too, is miraculously normal, and I am deeply grateful.

**Bring heaven to earth today
by watching the miracle of your baby in thanksgiving.**

Blessing and glory and wisdom and
thanksgiving and honor and power and
might be to our God forever and ever!
—Revelation 7:12

Anxiety

You would think I'm being paid to worry. Of course I worry about the normal things, like how soon to take the baby to the doctor when he's sick, and whether or not the house is sufficiently childproofed.

Lately, however, my worries are wandering all over my life! I worry about how soon my perfectly healthy baby will get sick again, and, if he gets chicken pox too early, how his poor little body will handle it. I worry that he will drown in a bucket of water when he's three or get hurt in a motorcycle accident when he's twenty. Maybe I should stop reading the paper. I can find enough to keep me anxious without all the added suggestions delivered to my doorstep every morning.

**God,
calm my soul
and let me take you up
on the offer to carry my worries for me.**

Cast all your anxiety on [God],
because he cares for you.

—I Peter 5:7

Creativity

I read somewhere that babies who have active involvement with their fathers are more creative. I think I finally figured out why that would be true.

If our family is typical of most—that the mother is with the baby more than the father—then I am probably typical of many mothers: completely out of creative energy by the end of the afternoon. I congratulate myself when I get supper made and the baby is still alive!

Then my husband comes swooping in from work, often tired, but not tired of being with a baby all day. He scoops her up, sings to her, and thinks of new games to play with her, just when my brain and arms are worn out. His presence brings new stimulation to both of us, and the more varied our stimulation, the more creative we can become!

**Thank God
for the strength of each adult in your baby's life.**

A wise child makes a glad father.
—Proverbs 10:1

Love from Others

I wish I could remember my days as an infant. Maria has had so many people bless her with their touch, caress her with their eyes, wrap her in their soft words, and give her a blanket of security with their love. I'm sure the same thing happened to me when I was a baby, but just as Maria won't know about all of those who aided her development, I don't know all who helped to lay my foundation either.

On the other hand, I don't really care to remember who all changed my diapers. Maybe God has a purpose in limiting our conscious memories!

**Thank you, God,
for all the unknown and forgotten people
who have nurtured me.**

On entering the house,
they saw the child with Mary his mother,
and they knelt down and paid him homage.
—Matthew 2:11

Nursing

Before I was pregnant, I knew that if I ever became a mother, I would want to nurse my baby. I figured it would be healthier and cheaper, and that was reason enough!

I never realized what a gift I'd be giving myself as well. When else would I stop the busyness of my day to sit down and simply hold the baby for fifteen to thirty minutes? How else would I force my body to relax, except to know that's the only way to get these mammary glands to produce?

Nursing is becoming a form of therapy for me. It helps me wake up in the morning, relaxes me during the day, and puts me to sleep at night.

**Enjoy the invitations
your baby gives you to slow down and relax.**

Out of the mouths of babes and infants
you have founded a bulwark.

—Psalm 8:2

Forgiveness

I knew I had to do something about those fingernails before he had scars all over his face and my arms. I also knew he would never let me trim them if the choice were his.

So I waited until he was asleep and then began to clip. Just when I was feeling successful in my plot, the clippers went farther than my eye. His screams and blood burst out at the same time.

I felt horrible. What kind of mother would wound her child while in his most vulnerable state? There must be a better way than the best I know!

That was my first clue that I could not be a perfect mother. I have had many other indications since. I only pray that this child will grow up with a spirit of forgiveness.

Where do you need
to forgive yourself?

For with the Lord there is steadfast love,
and with him is great power to redeem.

—Psalm 130:7

Morning Extrovert

This is the first time I've ever lived with someone with whom I cannot reason. I was always able to come to an understanding with my previous roommates that we wouldn't talk for at least the first hour of my day. One college roommate had a harder time getting used to that fact of my personality, but she was trainable, unlike the newest member of my household.

Maria wakes up jabbering every morning at 6 a.m. and somehow misses the fact that no one is talking back. All I want to do is play retractable turtle, but this new life is calling me to respond—if not dance—to her music!

**A mother's job
is to accept some unreasonableness.**

Joy comes with the morning.

—Psalm 30:5

Solitude

It took me a while to understand the meaning behind one particular cry of my baby. I learned the various cries of pain, fear, and discomfort fairly easily, and how to give her comfort. It took longer, however, to interpret the cry that no amount of cuddling or care could alleviate. I've come to believe it's her need for solitude!

I have to give up my storybook image of a baby who is merely a cuddly doll who breathes. She's a real person, who needs to have alone time to rejuvenate, just like I do.

Your baby's need for solitude is not rejection, but another aspect of growth.

At daybreak [Jesus] departed
and went into a deserted place.
—Luke 4:42

Body Image

I don't know from where it came, but a comforting thought swooped in to nurture my soul today. Not only is my baby made in the image of God (that's an easy connection), but so am I! Me, with my still-bulging belly, enlarged breasts, and energy that leaves long before the day is over. Suddenly, magazine images that dictate how a woman is supposed to look don't matter to me.

I've tended to look at people like Karen, whose slim body seemed to snap right back into shape the minute her baby was born, as a model toward which to strive. But there are lots of others who, like me, haven't made that elastic switch back. And I'm not wrong or bad—just different. All of these different bodies are included in "made in the image of God," fearfully and wonderfully!

**Look in a mirror and thank God
for whatever variation on the theme
"God's image" you see looking back.**

So God created humankind in his image.

—Genesis 1:27

Cabin Fever

That which can't be seen does not exist. The child development theories prepared me for this stage of babyhood, and I am fascinated watching it happen in real life. It's convenient to be able to hide a knife or marble, and, as soon as it's gone, my baby stops looking for it.

Sometimes I feel like I've regressed to that stage of infancy with him. I've been so wrapped up in being a mother that the rest of the world has disappeared. I don't see my options as clearly anymore, and it sometimes feels like none exist. I'm cloistered, and the overgrown walls are hiding the doors!

Go for a walk.

Let the light of your face shine on us,
O Lord!

—Psalm 4:6

Facing Limitations

Contrary to how I felt right after the baby was born, my energy has come back . . . a little. I thought I'd never be able to take care of this newborn *and* start cooking and exercising and working on a regular basis again.

I made it through the first six weeks, though, and now I keep expecting things to be normal. I want to be able to stay up until midnight. I want to do volunteer work. I want to stay in touch with friends.

But I'm still exhausted from getting up at least once during the night and again in the morning before I'm ready. I can't seem to get my own projects done. I feel disorganized and irresponsible. All of a sudden the week is over, and I haven't written one letter or called anyone just to catch up. These limitations are getting irritating!

When you become frustrated with not keeping up with responsibilities, think about all the new ones you've taken on since your baby's birth.

Give your strength to your servant.

—Psalm 86:16

Slow Down

Yesterday I felt so frustrated by my new limitations. When I think about my corresponding new responsibilities, however, my limits become gifts. When I can quiet myself and thank God for the gifts this baby has brought to me, I have a growing desire to relax and relish them.

When will I ever get a chance like this again: to have an excuse to sleep more than seems necessary, to say no to requests that make me too busy, to marvel quietly at life, rather than put it into endless words for others to hear? When will I ever get a better chance to focus on me and my beloved, to let peace and a zest for right living have time to flourish and grow within me?

**Where do righteousness and peace
kiss each other in your life?**

Steadfast love and faithfulness will meet;
righteousness and peace will kiss each other.
—Psalm 85:10

Wonder

My baby loves to lie on his back and look at the ceiling fan (well, for two minutes maybe). So I lay down beside him today to see what was so intriguing about it.

It was definitely a new way to look at the room. Everything seemed bigger, even to me. I wonder what it's like to be seeing all this for the first time and to have so little control over the movement around oneself.

I could use a renewal of wonder in my world and a reminder that my control is often an illusion. Maybe he was sent to me for this very purpose.

**Pray,
lying on your back today.**

Wonderful are your works;
   that I know very well.

—Psalm 139:14

Childcare

My first interview with a potential childcare provider was not my best performance. The grandmotherly woman was highly recommended by good friends, so, after meeting her, I was ready to talk about schedules. I didn't know what else to say.

"You could ask if I'm a Christian," she offered.

"Oh, right! Are you a Christian?" I asked dutifully.

"Yes." Silence followed.

"You could ask if I smoke."

"That's a good question. Do you smoke?"

"No."

She has turned out to be a blessing on Maria's little life. With her help, I now know many other questions that are important to have answered before I let my child in the arms of another. When I need to be away from the baby, having a loving, creative atmosphere for her helps me cope with my sadness in leaving.

**Thank God for the others
who love and care for your baby.**

Pharaoh's daughter said to her,
"Take this child and nurse it for me,
and I will give you your wages."
—Exodus 2:9

Object Constancy

I'm saddened when I leave Maria with someone else, because I know that at her stage of development, she doesn't understand that I will come back again. No wonder she cries when I leave! Then I'm upset, too. It's hard to go to work with a picture of her tearful face etched in my memory.

I waited outside the door the last time, though, to listen, and she quit crying almost as soon as the door closed. It helps to know that when I repeatedly leave her and return, she is developing a sense of stability in her world. It's still hard for both of us, though.

**God,
sometimes I feel like you've gone
and left me forever, too.
I'm grateful for the repeated proof of your constancy—
just like a mother's!**

Protect me,
O God, for in you I take refuge.

—Psalm 16:1

Faithfulness

I've heard that a man is prone to have an extramarital affair soon after the birth of his first child. While I think that's disgusting and don't want to believe it could happen to us, I can also see why it happens.

Sure, we have this precious new life in common, but much of what we used to have in common has been severely disrupted. We're both tired from broken nights so it takes more effort to listen to each other tell about our days or to stay awake long enough at night to discuss problems or to make love. On top of that, we're seeing a new side of ourselves and each other—parenthood—and discovering that our parenting styles are different. Our expectations of who does what, and how soon, need to be readjusted.

This baby cannot hold us together. Our history won't hold us together. We'll have to do it ourselves.

Love can always use a revival.

My beloved speaks and says to me:
"Arise, my love, my fair one, and come away."
—Song of Solomon 2:10

Hospitality

For the first five weeks after the baby was born, I didn't feel guilty about not having friends over for dinner. They were still bringing food to me! But soon after that, I started thinking it was time to return some of their hospitality!

It's not just that I feel guilty if I don't have guests. I want to have people over. It feels like more work than it used to be, though, so it's one of the things that just hasn't happened much these days.

This weekend we finally invited some friends who had us for dinner a year ago. I was feeling bad that it had taken us so long to return the favor, until, in the course of our conversation, she unapologetically said, "We've only had one other couple for a meal since you were there last year." Her baby is a year older than ours! Maybe I expect too much of myself.

**When you fall short of your expectations,
find someone different
with whom to compare yourself!**

May the God of steadfastness
and encouragement grant you to live
in harmony with one another.

—Romans 15:5

Inner Voice

I can't ever seem to complete my struggle to balance my roles, especially those of mother and career woman. I don't want to get stuck at home just because I'm a female. Nor do I want to play only the traditional male role just to prove I am equal to men.

Maybe there is no final answer. To live in the tension means I have to keep listening to my inner self. That, after all, is what women have traditionally done well. Maybe struggling for the right balance will be my way of life, rather than finding an answer once and for all.

**Cultivate your ability
to listen to your heart.**

You show me the path of life.
In your presence there is fullness of joy.
—Psalm 16:11

Mother Abuse

others
hood has changed me more than I am usually able to realize. Even my gut reactions have been altered. Before I was a mother, when I heard a child cry in the store or in a house I was walking by, my immediate thought was, "Child abuse!" I wondered what they were doing to that poor child.

Today I was walking down the street and heard a baby crying. My first response was, "Poor mother!"

**You may be more upset
by your baby's cries
than your baby is.**

Give ear to my word,
O Lord;
give heed to my sighing.

—Psalm 5:1

Selfishness

I never thought of myself as a selfish person. Never, that is, until my postpartum personality began to emerge!

When my baby was first born, I gave her all the time her care demanded, and I loved it. I still love her, of course, but I'm starting to grieve all the losses her life has meant for me as well.

I haven't had an uninterrupted conversation with a friend for months. When I go shopping I no longer have the luxury of thinking about the best buys, because my head is busy trying to keep the baby content long enough to get everything I need. I haven't worked at any of my hobbies, except reading an article every once in a while. The latest wrinkle is that we had to change our vacation plans because she got sick. Love has never been so hard. I hope it's true that the harder I work at something, the better it is.

**God,
fill me with your unselfish love.**

[Love] does not insist on its own way.
—I Corinthians 13:5

Crying

I met a grandmother in the grocery store today. Carrying an infant makes me an automatic, open target for everyone's remarks! We're all one big family now—me and all the other parents and grandparents with whom I brush shoulders but never before had cause to interact.

I felt her hot gaze at the very moment I wanted to disappear. No toy or nipple could quiet my baby, and I was about to leave my half-full cart right where it was and relieve the shoppers and clerks of our presence.

When I finally looked up apologetically, however, she was not glaring. She was smiling lovingly at my squalling baby. She said, "At least when he cries at night, you know where he is!"

**This, too,
will pass.**

Incline your ear to my cry.

—Psalm 88:2

Sleeping Peacefully

How long has it been since I went to bed and slept peacefully until I was ready to get up? Even before the baby was born, she took her cue for when to start kicking from my getting-ready-for-bed motions!

On the other hand, she no longer cries for hours when she wakes up, like during those first two months of her life. A little milk puts her back to sleep, and it usually doesn't take me long to follow. Maybe sleeping in peace doesn't have to mean uninterrupted sleep. It could mean accepting the rhythm of her sleep and deciding to be at peace with it. Maybe I can be exhausted and peaceful at the same time.

**When your baby wakens you tonight,
thank God for the life behind that cry!**

I will both lie down and sleep in peace.

—Psalm 4:8

Finding Balance

When my baby was born, I couldn't imagine leaving her. When I did have to go away the first time, I cried the whole way to work.

Now, however, when I find the right balance of time together and time apart, I know I'm a better mother than if I were home with her all the time. I feel refreshed and eager to be with her, even if it's cleaning up her messes. I think she also benefits by her interactions with another adult and children.

I find it helpful, too, to read about and watch and talk to other mothers. But no one else has my exact personality, needs, financial situation, gifts, energy, or baby. I have to listen to my baby, myself, and the God within me, to find the best balance for me.

**Thank you, God,
for the permission and encouragement to be myself.**

Thus says the Lord,
he who created you . . .
I have called you by name; you are mine.
—Isaiah 43:1

Perspective

Some days, or even weeks, seem senseless. For example, what was the use of this week? Maria was sick. She wasn't sick enough to be worried for her life, but sick enough to make me change all my plans. She needed to be away from other children, rest more, and be held and comforted a lot!

I finally got her cold by the end of the week, and then I was really miserable! I wanted someone to take care of me, but I was still the mother with a sick child. All I could think about was what a wasted week it was.

When I look at this week as one piece of the rest of my life, however, I see it as a tiny speck with a different sort of flavor—admittedly, sour. But some days (or weeks) are just like that.

**Perspective lends acceptance
and takes the necessity out of judgment.**

Enlarge the site of your tent,
and let the curtains of your habitations be stretched out.
—Isaiah 54:2

Perfection

Why do I so often focus on what I have yet to do, instead of enjoy how much I've gotten done? I remember one unkind remark longer than one hundred supportive ones. I let one mistake overshadow all my successes.

It certainly doesn't make me a happier person, and I don't expect this degree of perfection from anyone else. I'm acting like everything in my world is dependent on me. Thank goodness, it's not true!

**You don't have to be perfect
to be a good mother or a good person.**

It is better to take refuge in the Lord
than to put confidence in mortals.
—Psalm 118:8

Communication

Learning to communicate with my baby has helped me figure out why I don't like to visit on the phone. It's because I can't see facial expressions or body languages. I hear words and some emotion, but I can't see what the eyes are saying. I can't read what the other person's body is communicating. Sharing silence is the last thing I want to do over the phone.

My baby doesn't have words yet, but she surely can communicate! She kicks, her eyes plead or look away, her fingers reach, or she's still. Her body works together to let me know anger, happiness, contentment, irritation, and hunger.

Listening to anyone is enhanced by really looking at that person. I'll have to try it with my husband, too!

**Choose someone you love
and practice the art of listening.**

From the cloud there came a voice:
"This is my Son, the Beloved; listen to him!"
—Mark 9:7

Friends

I'm beginning to see some subtle yet definite changes in my friendships. I don't mean to drop friends, but it's been fun to be with different people who are also in this motherhood stage of life. It's easier to talk to another mother about the joys and exasperation of my new role, than to friends whose career or boyfriend is their priority.

I'm sure my single, childless, and grandparent-age friends don't mean to drop me either, but I'm simply not as available for spontaneous activities as I was several months ago.

It's hard to trust that my old, true friendships will endure this phase of my life, but I can hope.

**Call a friend you haven't seen lately
and think of something to ask about her life.**

May your friends be like the sun
as it rises in its might.

—Judges 5:31

Lack of Focus

Thank goodness, I never was one to do a project start-to-finish without interruption. I couldn't clean one room of the house or weed one row of the garden at a time. I'd do a little here and a little there, meandering through the messes. Or I'd zero in on the biggest pile of junk or the tallest weeds, and then move to the next one that caught my eye.

Seen as a lack of focus or weakness, it has suddenly become one of my main survival skills. I often only have time to clean up the worst messes. Major projects that require uninterrupted blocks of time, like cleaning out the refrigerator, will have to wait until my mother comes to visit!

**Thank you, God,
for the new perspective on some of my quirks.**

Young men and women alike,
old and young together!
Let them praise the name of the Lord.

—Psalm 148:12, 13

Growing Child

The thing that has always bothered me about our dog is that he can't anticipate much, except that when I open a certain cupboard door, he's going to get supper. He never shares my excitement about my birthday, or that it might snow tomorrow.

Our baby can't anticipate much yet either, but that won't last long. She already seems to be respecting the fact that I don't talk first thing in the morning. She doesn't babble quite as much as she used to. She gets excited when I get the backpack out to go for a walk. And she already has a favorite color. She always waits until the blue balloon comes around on her mobile to swing at it. What a wonder to watch her grow.

**Thank God
for the development of your baby.**

And Jesus increased in wisdom
and in years, and in divine and human favor.

—Luke 2:52

Blessings

Today, looking at this beautiful, healthy baby lying next to me, I am overwhelmed with the goodness of my life. I think of other mothers and babies in the world who don't have as much as I do of safety, love, and security. A survivor's guilt begins to creep in. What right do I have to so many blessings?

Answering those thoughts of guilt is what I believe is the voice of God, saying that we all deserve to be clothed, fed, and loved. Everyone doesn't get what they deserve, but if I don't enjoy my blessings, that's only one more person not getting what she deserves.

**Bask
in your blessings.**

Listen carefully to me,
and eat what is good,
and delight yourselves in rich food.

—Isaiah 55:2

Blessing Returned

After I basked in the blessings of my life yesterday, I felt flooded. So much has been given to me that I have to return some of it to God, to my family, to the world!

Suddenly I have extra energy and direction to pray for others. I started planning a celebration supper to share with some friends. I went for a walk and stopped to talk to a few neighbors. It's not that profound, really, and yet I didn't even have this much to give until I let God nurture me for a day!

**The next time you buy something for your baby,
buy the same thing for another baby
who wouldn't get it otherwise.**

So shall my word be
that goes out from my mouth;
it shall not return to me empty.

—Isaiah 55:11

Work

Every time someone asks me what I'm doing these days, I talk about my social work job. Even though I only do that for one or two days a week, that's what I say, because that's what I think they're asking. Behind the question I hear other silent ones: "What are you doing to make money? How are you proving your worth professionally?"

When am I going to have enough nerve to start answering that question by telling them about my main job? Mothering doesn't earn money, but it is a difficult and priceless vocation. Society's definition of work has got to change. Maybe it will start with my own attitude!

**Expand the "work" in today's verse,
to *all* your work.**

Commit your work to the Lord.

—Proverbs 16:3

The Honeymoon Is Over

I think we're past the honeymoon stage! Yes, we still love the baby and each other, but I've never seen this side of my husband before, nor of myself, for that matter. Back in the good old days, several months ago, when we had a conflict between us, we mulled it over for a few days until we could talk about it with less emotion and at least a little tact.

Suddenly, however, our differences flare up quickly. We need to know, right now, whether we are going to pick the baby up or let her put herself back to sleep. Can she go to church barefoot today? Is she sick enough to call the doctor? There's no time to let our opinions simmer. We have to learn how to live together all over again!

**Give your wisdom,
Lord,
to the meshing of our convictions.**

How very good and pleasant it is
when kindred live together in unity!

—Psalm 133:1

147

The Wardrobe

I remember feeling overwhelmed by the task of supplying a whole wardrobe for the new little member of our family. That was before the baby showers and the hand-me-downs started pouring in. Then I was overwhelmed by the generosity of our friends, and I laughed in disbelief as I held up each tiny outfit.

Last night I found a box of clothes under the crib that seemed much too big two months ago when I stuck them out of the way. I forgot they were there, and now they're too little! I don't know whether to be disappointed that I missed seeing all those cute clothes on her, or to laugh at my previous worries about having enough. She obviously has plenty!

Give thanks for all who have helped to clothe your baby.

Consider the lilies of the field,
how they grow; they neither toil nor spin.
Yet I tell you, even Solomon in all his glory
was not clothed like one of these.
—Matthew 6:28, 29

Miracles

I am surrounded by miracles. Every day I see my baby learning new things that I take for granted, but which look fresh and amazing as I watch him experiment and finally succeed. His uncoordinated hands hit a swinging toy, and I watch as he trains them to do it again with purpose. He reaches for the rainbow reflected on the floor, but can't pick it up. Last night he cried with fear when he saw his shadow in front of him. He tries to get that voice out of the phone so he can see his daddy. He's learned that scrunching up his nose makes me laugh.

I can almost see his brain working, figuring. Miracles permeate life as never before. Maybe they've always been here and I've just slowed down enough to notice them.

**Watch for the free
and constant demonstration
of miracles your baby provides.**

Great is the Lord,
and greatly to be praised.

—Psalm 145:3

149

Adjustment

I can't believe how fast my feelings change! One minute I'm feeling content and as though my life is finally becoming manageable. Then the phone rings. A friend wonders if I can listen to a lonely person who just had a baby. He assures me I'd be so good for her, so of course I melt to his affirmation. "Oh that would be fun!" I manage to say, which it would be, but . . .

Then I hang up the phone, and my stomach twists my belly button to my spine and my shoulders engulf my neck in tension. What am I doing? I don't even have the time and energy to be with the friends I already have! It's so hard to adjust to the depleted energy levels of living with a baby.

**When God gives you contentment,
let yourself relax in it before you
allow the needs of others to wear
down your energies again.**

The Lord will feed his flock like a shepherd;
he will gather the lambs in his arms,

and carry them in his bosom,
and gently lead the mother sheep.

—Isaiah 40:11

Laundry

"You must love to wash clothes!" The neighbor's off-hand remark, as he passed me at the washline on his way to work, left me, for once, without a reply.

Love to wash clothes? No, I wouldn't say that. I don't hate it either, but I don't search the house every morning, hoping to find enough dirty laundry to constitute a load!

Actually, I used to hate it. An overflowing laundry basket was one of my chronic problems. Then I heard another mother say she does one load a day. What a violation of my mother's tradition. Monday and Thursday are washdays.

I decided to try my friend's method anyway, and it works. One load a day doesn't take much effort and it goes a long way in relieving the stress of the pile that never ends. Plus, every once in a while I get a day off because there's not enough laundry for a load. (I'll bet the neighbor man doesn't notice!)

Take pride and find joy in your mini-steps.

The boundary lines have fallen for me in pleasant places.

—Psalm 16:6

Laundry Continues

Yesterday my laundry confessions seemed so neat and well planned. To keep me humble, I have to keep an honest record. Today's load didn't get hung up until 10 p.m.! (My mother would have never done this!) I guess I'll let that double as tomorrow's load, too.

God,
thanks for helping me to find
new definitions for my accomplishments.

I bless the Lord who gives me counsel;
in the night also my heart instructs me.

—Psalm 16:7

Possessiveness

I don't know whether to feel relieved or jealous. When I dropped my son off at Cindy's today on my way to work, he went right to her without even looking back to watch me go. He could have acted like he'd miss me a little.

On the other hand, I'm glad he feels close to another mother figure. John's and my love for him frees him to branch out with his love. I haven't noticed that he has any less for me after he gives some of it away. Maybe this is similar to generations past when mothers often shared childcare with neighboring relatives. It's helpful to think of family as stretching beyond the bounds of my biological family.

**Thank you, God,
that my son is already broadening
his circle of love and trust.**

Then Naomi took the child
and laid him in her bosom,
and became his nurse.

—Ruth 4:16

Home

After a long day of work my husband worked his way carefully through the toy-strewn living room to the mess I was keeping company with in the kitchen. With a satisfied sigh and a kiss, he said, "This home looks lived in."

What a refreshing way to look at the remainders of the day's activities! Why do I work so hard to get all the visual evidence put away before he comes home, and then tell him what we did all day? He can get the full picture this way.

**Redefining a problem
is a helpful coping mechanism.**

"Martha, Martha,
you are worried and distracted by many things;
there is need of only one thing."
—Luke 10:41, 42

Love Languages

I feel incredibly loved today. John knew I was tired last evening, so he made supper, did the dishes, and got up with Maria several times through the night when she cried with sore gums. Nothing makes me feel so loved as when he does things for me.

I know other people feel most loved when they are given time together or gifts or words of love. John, like many men, hears my love the loudest when I touch him. Of course I usually forget and show my love for him with *my* love language—doing things. Then I get upset when he doesn't appreciate it enough. I'll have to remember to touch him when he comes home tonight.

Recognize your husband's love language, then test it with him to see if you're right.

My beloved is mine and I am his.
—Song of Solomon 2:16

Money

Every time we get a paycheck, I hurry to pay all the bills that are due before we get paid again. I love to have enough money to pay them and sometimes even put a little into savings. I worry if I don't know how something will get paid. I'm too tired at night to do most things, but reviewing the budget keeps me wide awake, figuring and contriving. What will go where? Do I need to work more? Could I work less?

It must be the parenting instinct that is taking control of me! I don't remember thinking about money so much before we had a child. The line between providing adequately for the baby and being a miser seems harder than ever to keep in sight.

**God,
help me enjoy my possessions
without them possessing me.**

Keep your lives free from the love of money.
—Hebrews 13:5

Dashed Expectations

I still cannot fathom how this baby is taking so much of my time! I see it happen every day, and every night I'm still surprised how much is left to do on a list that I thought was modest-sized.

I have moments of inspiration during which I understand that mothering an infant is a full-time job. For the most part, however, I still think of it as a hobby to work in alongside all my other interests. It's no wonder I'm surprised every evening!

**Try a day with nothing on your to-do list,
except taking care of your baby.**

Return, O my soul,
to your rest,
for the Lord has dealt bountifully with you.
—Psalm 116:7

Self-Acceptance

Part of the reason it's so hard for me to accept the amount of time the baby takes is that I assume others don't understand. If I were my husband, gone to work all day and coming home to this messy house, no supper started, dirty diapers halfway to the pail, and the dog needing to be walked, I'd wonder what my wife had been doing all day!

It must all be inside my head, though, because he's never even hinted at that attitude. He just picks our baby up, hugs us both, and tells me what a wonderful mother I am.

**Let your heart enjoy
the compliments of others,
instead of telling them why they're wrong.**

You are altogether beautiful,
my love;
there is no flaw in you.
—Song of Solomon 4:7

Nursery Rhyme Violence

Tonight I held my daughter in the rocker and sang lullabies as she drifted off to sleep. Suddenly I heard myself singing, ". . . when the bough breaks, the cradle will fall and down will come baby, cradle, and all." What horrible words with that soothing music! She can't understand them yet, but someday she will.

I'm starting to review everything in a new light now—the light of motherhood. I may as well start right away so it will come easier by the time she understands what she hears and sees.

I start again and this time I sing, ". . . and I will catch baby, cradle, and all." You are safe with me, baby.

**Rewrite
the violence in
your favorite nursery rhyme.**

Oh Lord my God,
in you I take refuge.

—Psalm 7:1

God's Faithfulness

I was blaming the baby for the interruption of my prayer life. I excused myself from scripture meditation and study because of my exhaustion. I justified my lapse in spending time with God alone, since I've added so many responsibilities to my life.

At first I easily rationalized the changes. Eventually I knew it had gone on for too long. Later still, I was too embarrassed to admit my absence, even to God. Finally, I couldn't stay away any longer.

And suddenly I knew—God was here the whole time! I don't have to go back. I can just be *here* with God.

**I've missed you, God.
Thank you for not leaving.**

On the day I called,
you answered me;
you increased my strength of soul.

—Psalm 138:3

My Faithfulness

After rediscovering God's faithfulness yesterday and thanking God for not leaving me, I thought how silly I had been. Of course God doesn't leave me when I'm tired. God doesn't give up on me when our regular meeting times are interrupted by a change in routine. God doesn't go away when I am overwhelmed with my new life.

Would I do that to my baby? I can't imagine not loving this child, even as she becomes more independent, even though she will probably tell me she hates me, even when she leaves home. And since I'm made in God's image, it makes sense that God always loves me, too.

**Watch for how your baby
shows you more of God.**

[I] give thanks to your name
for your steadfast love and your faithfulness.
—Psalm 138:2

Learning

A friend visited today and, in a rare gesture of love, offered to change my baby's diaper. I heard her tell him to be patient because she couldn't do it as fast as his mama. That caught my attention because as far as Jonathan is concerned, his mama doesn't change it fast enough either. Having no one else to give me feedback, I had simply believed him. I was the world's slowest diaper changer.

I watched, however, and, sure enough, my friend stumbled around like I remember doing at first. I never noticed my improvement. Seeing the comparison now, I realize that I have become more efficient, speedy, and neat in this oft-repeated, important task of our days. How nice to know!

**Thank you, God,
for my increasing ease in mothering.**

Do not forsake the work of your hands.

—Psalm 138:8

Crying

I caught a friend crying today. I could tell she was embarrassed for me to find her that way, but since she couldn't hide it, she told me why she was upset. Then she asked me if I ever cry. Knowing I do seemed to make her feel better.

Admitting it to her made me think about how little I let others see my tears. In my head I know it's okay to cry, but I don't readily show it or talk about it. I find it comforting, though, to know other people cry, too. Maybe that's what John, the disciple, knew when he told us about Jesus's tears, and what translators understood when they gave that revelation a verse all to itself.

**Jesus,
it's comforting to know that you cried, too.**

Jesus began to weep.

—John 11:35

Guilt

Guilt isn't a new thing for me. I've often felt guilty about what I do and guilty about what I don't do. Mother Guilt, however, is a new feeling and its power is disconcerting! It comes uninvited and isn't easily dismissed.

I feel like I give some days either to feeling guilty, rationalizing my actions, or letting guilt creep back for its next attack. I feel guilty when I'm with the baby so much that I get irritated with her, blaming her will for stubbornness and her curiosity for disobedience. Then I feel guilty when I leave her.

Do "Mother" and "Guilt" have to go together? I want to be a good mother, but who defines that? If I try to live up to what I think everyone else expects of me, the two words probably will go together. Maybe it's a big enough job to be the mother I decide to be.

**Believe in your goodness
as a person, as a mother.**

There is therefore now no condemnation
for those who are in Christ Jesus.

—Romans 8:1

Bored

Today I heard myself think, "I'm bored." It surprised me because "bored" is not a part of the vocabulary I've ever used to describe myself. I don't like when I feel it in connection with mothering. It's true, though. I do feel bored.

It's not that I sit around wondering what to do. I could think of plenty of fun things to do if I were alone. I'm always busy, too, but it's this new kind of busyness, taking care of the needs of an infant, that gets boring. I feel trapped by her limitations. She's too young to enjoy the Children's Museum, doesn't eat the food I'd pack for a picnic, and can't help me bake cookies.

Raising a child is not all fun and games. That's just the part we parents put in the photo albums.

**Plan something fun for yourself
and savor your enjoyment.**

What do people gain from all the toil
at which they toil under the sun?
—Ecclesiastes 1:3

Enjoying the Present

At the grocery store yesterday I saw a woman, obviously pregnant, leisurely comparing prices. I was instantly jealous. I remembered the contentment of being in a crowd yet being enthralled with the interior world I couldn't share: receiving those kicks from inside that no one else knew about, and rubbing back. I had the luxury of my baby's presence, while being alone for all practical purposes, doing whatever I wanted, whenever I wanted.

My baby's screams brought me back to my present reality. The rattle I brought had lost its attraction. She didn't want any more of the crackers I was buying for immediate gratification.

Yes, those were the days. But then, that woman is probably nervous about labor and delivery!

**Whatever stage I'm in,
there's something to give up and something to gain.**

. . . a time to plant and a time to pluck up what is planted.
—Ecclesiastes 3:2

Friendship

I got a wretched phone call from a friend last night. All in one breath she said I never call her to ask how she's doing anymore, I haven't invited her over for dinner in ages, and she wonders if I even want to be her friend anymore. I started feeling bad, wondering how I could have let our friendship slide like I have.

But then I remembered a call I recently received from another friend. She said she misses me, but knows I can't be as available right now with a new baby. She just wanted to remind me of her love.

This new friendship I'm cultivating with my baby has obviously taken precedence. I'm sorry it alters all my other relationships, but my real friends will still be there when I've adjusted to this change and have more time and initiative again. It's hard for me to remember that life will not always be like it is at this very moment.

**Lord, help me to be patient with myself,
even when my friends aren't.**

A true friend sticks closer than one's nearest kin.
—Proverbs 18:24

Love

I wish I could remember, forever, all the people who have come to hold, to love, and to bless our baby. For such a young life, she has already had an incredible amount of love and nurturing poured into her soul. I am sad when I realize that some of the friends and relatives who have loved her the most have already moved out of her life.

I know, however, that her personality and character are already being formed. When she cries and I respond, she learns to trust. When I let others hold her, she learns that she can let go of me and I will come back. When she is loved, she learns to love. When she is held gently, she learns to be gentle. She will live out of what she receives even now.

No act or word of love is ever lost.

Train children in the right way,
and when old,
they will not stray.

—Proverbs 22:6

Too Much Advice

"I just listen politely, thank them for their wisdom, then go home and do whatever you want to do!" Having a baby seems to make everyone think I want to hear their favorite theory on how to raise children. Here was one more piece of advice about all the advice that sometimes sends me reeling. I like this one, though. With it, I could satisfy the people-pleasing part of me, yet keep the power myself! I could benefit from the opinions of others, while reclaiming my own wisdom and intuition.

Sometimes I lose sight of the fact that God has given me the gift of motherhood. I can know that God will continue to be my guide.

**Resources are just that—resources,
not a replacement for my innate capabilities.**

But Mary treasured all these words
and pondered them in her heart.

—Luke 2:19

Nursing

When he started crying at bedtime, the baby didn't seem to care about my cuddling arms. My lovely singing didn't quiet him. He didn't even look at my face. He focused lower and then dived! All he wanted was my milk.

I could feel my body being drained. I felt like he was sucking away at my very being. When he finally got his fill and went to sleep, I had to lie down myself to be replenished—soul and body.

I wonder if he can tell when I'm giving milk to him freely and when he has to take it? I enjoy it more when I give out of my plenty, both of love and of milk. There is little pleasure when I feel my energy draining into the little body in my arms. Those are the days I feel like a cow. Hook me up to my little calf and let him suck me dry. But some days are just cow days.

God, thank you for not going "cow" on me.

The Lord is my strength and my might.
—Psalm 118:14

Self-Worth

Some days I feel the strength of motherhood running through my veins and muscles, pulling me to heights I never knew before. The house lights up in wonder.

Other days the mere thought of being a mother wears me out. The drudgery of repeated dishes, laundry, diapers, cleaning, etc., etc. looms like a dark cloud over the house.

Then I realized that my attitude is often affected by whom I'm around or what I'm reading. I'm disgusted at how quickly my sense of self-worth can be influenced by others. So I have two choices. I can surround myself with people who have uplifting attitudes, or build my own within. If I'm able, doing both would be a good insurance plan!

Remember in whose image you are created.

The Lord will arise upon you,
and his glory will appear over you.
—Isaiah 60:2

Claustrophobic

Living with this baby is starting to feel claustrophobic! My bed used to be a haven of rest. I had most of my friends trained not to call me after 10 p.m., preferably not after nine.

But now my on-call shifts are never over. No time of night is sacred. Even when it's my husband's turn to get up with the baby, my body tenses with the first cry and has a hard time relaxing again. This is no longer a home of rest.

I want a turn at being rocked and cuddled and fed. I'd even settle for an hour of guaranteed silence, outside of these walls, to sip a cup of hot chocolate.

**Treat yourself to some guaranteed silence
and imagine God or your husband repeating
the following verse to you while you rest
in their arms like a baby.**

How beautiful you are,
my love,
how very beautiful.

—Song of Solomon 4:1

Openness

Yesterday one of my best friends told me her daughter was causing trouble at school. The teachers were asking her to think about placing the child in a private school where she would be given more attention.

I was shocked! I had no idea she was having any problems. It took a crisis for her to admit aloud that her daughter was anything less than perfect.

I wonder why we parents work so hard at hiding problems. I am disappointed in friends who don't admit the hard part of parenting. I feel lonely in my problems when my friends don't reciprocate honestly with theirs. Do I ever project an image of no problems, too?

**Thank God for the friends who,
in their openness, allow you to be open as well.**

Whoever speaks the truth gives honest evidence,
but a false witness speaks deceitfully.
—Proverbs 12:17

Home

Why is it that I never realize how smudged my glasses are until I'm out in public? How can I smell like sour milk and not notice the stains accumulating on my clothes at home, but wilt from self-consciousness if a drop spills on me at work? Why is "playing" on my job description as a mother, but reason to dock my pay as a social worker?

Maybe it's because at home I'm loved for who I am, more than what I look like or what I do. The total acceptance I receive from my family reflects God's love to me on an everyday basis. How refreshing to come home!

**Thank you, God,
for putting skin on your love,
in the form of my family.**

[Her husband] praises her:
"Many women have done excellently,
but you surpass them all."
—Proverbs 31:28, 29

Responsibility

Some days I feel like I'm playing house. The fact that my baby is more than a doll seems insignificant. I forget, momentarily, about paying bills, meeting deadlines, or planning meals beyond the afternoon tea party.

Today, however, is not one of those days. I've been hit with the gravity of my situation. This child is already learning from me. My mannerisms, tone of voice, attitudes, and spirituality cannot be hidden from this tiny, growing individual. I know she will make her own decisions eventually. Until then, however, I am one of her main role models.

**Help me,
God.**

Hear, my child,
your father's instruction,
and do not reject your mother's teaching.
—Proverbs 1:8

Whom Does He Look Like?

People are always trying to figure out whom our baby looks like. All of the people on my side of the family think he looks like me. His paternal relatives remember his father's baby pictures when they see him. But when I'm alone with him, strangers say, "He must look like his dad." When he's with his dad alone, even good friends who haven't seen him for a while say, "Whose baby are you holding?"

Yesterday, after one of those familiar discussions about whom our son will look like, a quiet nonparticipant in the judging said, "Maybe he'll just look like Jonathan." What a relief!

Free your baby
from as many boxes as possible.

When Adam had lived 130 years,
he became the father of a son in his likeness,
according to his image.

—Genesis 5:3

Fear of Death

Absence makes the heart grow fonder. I have never felt the truth of that adage more than when I am gone from my baby. Yesterday when I was away, I heard sirens blowing. I looked out to see a funeral procession going by. My stomach immediately hurt—not with pain for that family, but wondering how I would cope if the sirens were blowing for my husband or child. Panic grabbed me before I could remind myself that they are safe. Why do I worry about things that haven't happened?

When I saw them again last night, they were more precious than ever. The depth of my love was resurrected, and I took nothing for granted, at least for the next ten minutes.

**Look at your baby
as if you've been apart for a week.**

While he was still far off,
his father saw him and was filled with compassion;
he ran and put his arms around him and kissed him.

—Luke 15:20

Self-Approval

Of course I can understand that my baby cannot thank me for all the work I do for her. But sometimes I wish she would just let me change her diaper without wiggling and screaming as if I were torturing her. I wish I could get an evaluation on my job performance; I'd like to hear someone say how well I'm doing, followed by a merit increase in salary! A lunch break would improve my attitude for the afternoon ahead.

Pre-motherhood, I relied on a paycheck as my concrete approval of a job well done. I guess I'll have to learn to approve of myself.

**Lord,
help me to account for the efforts of motherhood,
even when they're invisible.**

When you pass through the waters,
I will be with you . . .
and the flame shall not consume you.
For I am the Lord your God.

—Isaiah 43:2, 3

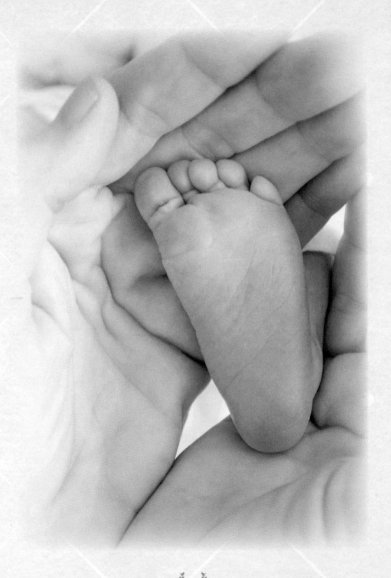

Marriage

Yesterday I had a strange experience in the restroom of a restaurant! A woman I didn't even know began telling me about a couple she saw on television. She described them by saying they were still in their first marriage.

I don't know what else she said because I never got past that comment. It strikes me as incredibly sad that a couple in their first marriage is odd enough to have that be the defining point of their identity.

It's making me think about how much I want that to be my identity, too, for *my* stability as well as that of my baby.

My child will know she is safe
when she sees me loving her dad.

Let marriage be held in honor by all.
—Hebrews 13:4

Broken Marriage

As much as I want to stay married always to John, and want all my friends and relatives to have everlastingly stable marriages, I also know the reality. It simply doesn't happen for everyone. And if I believe children find stability in the stability of their parents' marriage, where does brokenness leave them?

I am amazed at the flexibility of children. I want all children—no matter their parents' marital situation—to know that adult brokenness is not their fault. Even if the brokenness in our house doesn't lead to divorce, but to a day of bad feelings, I want my child to know she's loved and blameless.

**God, help me to be aware of my child's
growing awareness and respond to her feelings,
even when I'm nearly overwhelmed with my own.**

The Lord is near to the brokenhearted,
and saves the crushed in spirit.

—Psalm 34:18

Enthusiasm

One of the delights of watching the baby has been seeing how his whole body responds when he's happy. With every new discovery his face lights up, he squeals, and his arms and legs all wiggle at the same time. His enthusiasm for simple pleasures, like his first taste of ice cream or a squeaky toy, is pure joy.

I realize how long it's been since I have been so totally enthusiastic about anything. I've been too tired and responsible and practical to pull out all the stops on exuberance. I have so much to learn from this, my role model in joy!

What would you need to add or remove from your life to experience a moment of exhilarating joy?

The joy of the Lord is your strength.
—Nehemiah 8:10

Homeschooling

There's a lot of talk in my circle of friends these days about homeschooling. Many plan to try it. My first reaction is that I'm not a teacher, and my child will get a much better education by going to a regular school.

I've also heard, however, that children learn half of all they will ever know by the time they're three years old. If that's true, I'm already homeschooling! I am my child's first and main teacher, whether or not I'm trained and whether or not I'm aware of it. What a frightening thought.

The attitudes and values I want my child to have will need to flow naturally out of who I am. Teaching will not stop in the evening when I'm tired or the one time I make an exception to my honesty. My baby is already absorbing much learning in his most natural school— our home.

**God,
help me to be a wise,
aware, and consistent teacher.**

Keep these words that I am commanding you today in your heart. Recite them to your children and talk about them when you are at home and when you are away, when you lie down and when you rise.

—Deuteronomy 6:6, 7

Blessings

One thing I can no longer hear, since becoming a mother, is knowing of mothers who are too poor to feed their babies. I can't imagine the pain of having a hungry baby and not having food for her.

Even worse is an attitude I heard from a nine-year-old's lips last week. He said he'll never be poor because he's smart. Maybe I didn't want to hear that because I tend to act out that same attitude, even though I know many people are poor through no fault of their own. Working hard to support myself, it's easy to assume I deserve my blessings because I earn them.

Lord, help me to receive and appreciate the blessings you give without either undue feelings of guilt for all I have or improper feelings of earning what I've received.

The race is not to the swift . . . nor bread
to the wise, nor riches to the intelligent . . .
but time and chance happen to them all.
—Ecclesiastes 9:11

Listening

I'm continually grateful for the friends I have who will listen to me—especially the ones who don't judge me or assume I'll think the same way tomorrow. I often need to figure out what I think and feel by saying it aloud. I learn to know myself better by hearing what I say to friends who listen without needing to change me.

Listening in this way is not easy or to be taken for granted. Every mother would do well to have at least one such friend, but not be bitter about the limited supply.

**God,
help me to use the gift of listening,
with my friends and with my child as she grows.**

Let everyone be quick to listen,
slow to speak.

—James 1:19

Unplanned Pregnancy

Talking to a friend today, I was reminded that not everyone who has a baby planned to have one, nor even wanted one. My friend said when she found out she was pregnant, she cried for weeks. She didn't have time for a baby. She didn't have enough money, and she didn't feel strong enough to support anyone's psychological, physical, emotional, or spiritual needs beyond her own. The worst part was that she didn't think anyone would understand, so she kept her pain to herself.

I wish I had known. I wanted to get pregnant, and, even so, I had plenty of doubts and questions as I watched my belly grow. I can understand how an unplanned pregnancy would set your whole world off-balance! Everyone, it seems, sees babies as a blessing, but to the unprepared mother, they can feel like a burden.

Sharing doubts and questions can reduce the pain and provide ways to cope.

If one member suffers, all suffer together with it.

—I Corinthians 12:26

Support

One of the things I still remember and appreciate about my parents is that I never heard them tell anyone else anything bad about their children. I heard other people confide negative things about their children to my parents, but stories about me were never reciprocated.

I didn't grow up thinking my parents considered me to be perfect. I did grow up, however, knowing my parents loved me more than anyone else, along with my sister and brothers, and would do anything they could for me. I knew they were proud of me and wouldn't betray me, even to make themselves look good.

My parents let me know I could count on their love and support by what they didn't say. I hope I can give my children the same restraint.

Listen to how you talk to others about your baby. Someday your child will be able to understand.

Make me to know your ways, O Lord;
teach me your paths.

—Psalm 25:4

Discipline

I've been thinking about discipline lately, realizing it's easier to decide how to handle a situation before I'm suddenly smack in the middle of it. It's also easier to evaluate what I like or don't like about how others discipline their children before I'm in the throes of dealing with my own child who's misbehaving.

I know I want to let my child be free to become her own person instead of my clone. In her freedom, though, I want her to feel safety in knowing I'm in charge, so she doesn't have the weight of the world on her shoulders at three years of age.

Two pieces of advice make sense to me. I've heard my parents say, "Make as few rules as possible, just ones that will ensure safety." Another friend advises refraining from the word "No" whenever possible. Try not to say "No" to anything that won't matter in five years. Now, let's see if I can do it, at least on my good days!

**Thoughtful decisions on discipline now
will feel better than reacting out of frustration later.**

Do not withhold discipline
from your children.

—Proverbs 23:13

Irritation

I've never known anybody to sweat so profusely and care so little about it as this baby! I know she doesn't have much choice about whether or not she's in front of the fan or in air-conditioning, but she doesn't seem irritated by the beads of sweat standing on her lip and rolling down her cheeks.

I wonder if I am especially irritated with the summer heat, because I'm receiving what I think I don't deserve. I have a long list of irritating triggers, from rained-out hikes, to broken promises. My baby's list, on the contrary, is quite basic. She's irritable when she's uncomfortable, hungry, or tired. I wish I had that short a list.

**Think of your most recent source of irritation.
Do you need to resolve it or accept it?**

I have learned to be content
with whatever I have.

—Philippians 4:11

Love

I was so afraid I wouldn't be a good mother. When my sister had her first baby, I spent a weekend with them. It wasn't until I was on my way home that I realized I hadn't even offered to hold the child. When I later apologized, my sister said it was okay. She hadn't expected me to! Everyone said I'd like my own baby, but I asked friends to pray to that end, because I wasn't at all sure.

That memory seems strange now. The miracle of bonding happened so fast and has lasted so continuously that I sometimes forget my fear of motherhood. The love I've been given to give away is astounding every time I consider it.

**Thank you, God,
for letting me experience so great a love,
in receiving and in giving.**

. . . let her who bore you rejoice.

—Proverbs 23:25

Unique

Before I had a child, I had my theory of children down pat. After careful study of the options, I believed that, for the most part, children learn how to act and react by what they see in the people around them. Behavior is learned. Personalities are chosen.

But then my daughter came out kicking. Actually, even before she was born, she dug into my ribs and stayed there, no matter how much I tried to massage her back into place. From the start she did not cuddle in order to be comforted. Before I was ready, she preferred the bottle to the breast, apparently so she could look around while she drank. She came alive in a crowd and loved parties.

I still believe I am to be a model for her in learning social etiquette, faith values, and appropriate behavior. Much of who she will be, however, seems to have started before I had a chance to teach!

God, I'm glad you're the One in control here!

> O Lord, how manifold are your works!
> In wisdom you have made them all.
> —Psalm 104:24

Blessed

I feel overwhelmingly blessed today. On days like this, I know that I'm blessed every day, but what a bonus when the knowledge is joined by the feelings.

I can't really say what's different about today. The sunshine helps, I'm sure, as do our plans to eat out tonight. I don't feel like trying to analyze it. I will simply rest in the pleasure of feeling blessed, because when I do, I treasure my baby more, I love my husband more fully, I value myself more highly, and the world is a lovelier place to be.

**God,
I offer you a huge and simple
"Thank you!"**

I will give thanks to the Lord with my whole heart.
—Psalm 9:1

Scattered

I was complaining to one of my mentors that I feel completely scattered. There's too much to do and too little time in which to do it. Refusing to enter my hysteria, he said, "But you know how to juggle. You've been doing it for years."

I guess he's right. Adding another full-time job—caring for a growing baby—is just one more ball in the scheme of life. It's a big one, but if I give myself credit for all I've already learned to juggle—gardening, managing coupons, entertaining, organizing the household, meal preparation, reading, cleaning, paying the bills on time, praying, mending, as well as jobs that pay—I can handle one more.

**Encourage another mother
in all the "balls" she's juggling.**

But my eyes are turned toward you,
O God, my Lord:
in you I seek refuge; do not leave me defenseless.
—Psalm 141:8

Fear

This morning's newspaper confirmed my fear. The gun-shot I heard as I was going to bed last night fatally hit a man in our neighborhood.

I wonder if it was one of the guys I've seen on my daily walk with the stroller past the corner. Was it a drug deal? A family argument? My parents will think we live in a dangerous neighborhood.

I know it can happen anywhere. The fact is, though, bad news doesn't roll off my shoulders like it did before my baby was born. Fear lodges deeper within me now that my life is more than just me.

Jesus,
I need your indwelling peace more than ever.

Immediately [Jesus] spoke to them and said,
"Take heart, it is I; do not be afraid."

—Mark 6:50

Vacation

I was dreaming about vacations the other day and how I've always looked forward to breaking from the routine, getting away from home, and relaxing in the lack of responsibilities. That's what vacations used to be, anyway.

Mothering, as far as I can tell, doesn't offer "vacation" in its benefit package. We can go, but the demands away from home rise with the mileage. We pack half the house and still have to stop at the first grocery store to replace the apple juice we left on the kitchen counter. Instead of enjoying the countryside we're driving through, I'm shaking every rattle in the bag and trying to convince John it's my turn to drive. By the time we're settled for the night, my eyes won't stay open to gaze at the first star. Vacations have become a complicated variation on the theme, Mothering.

**Redefine "vacation"
and it might yet be saved!**

She . . . does not eat the bread of idleness.
—Proverbs 31:27

Time-Absorbing

I used to think I didn't have time for children. My schedule already had too little free time for relaxing or reading or taking walks. There was no extra time when I could care for a child.

Now childcare is my way of life! I miss some of the adult-only activities and free time, but there are other parts of life I could not have known without this child chapter.

To know my child is to marvel at the new depth of my love and new understanding of God's love. She shows me a new perspective as I watch her discover, learn, and remember. When I'm with her and when I'm not, I am no longer a person in isolation. She is part of me and I am part of her. She takes all of my time, which is exactly what I have to give.

**Thank you, God, for the gift of this new way of life.
Grant to me the grace to enjoy it today.**

For we are what he has made us,
created in Christ Jesus for good works,
which God prepared beforehand to be our way of life.
—Ephesians 2:10

201

Holy Home

"You're not pregnant anymore, but you're still barefoot and in the kitchen!" My friend laughed, but I didn't. I'm not enjoying my kitchen duties today. I don't like the implications of that slogan either, that women are only good for taking care of the house and making babies.

Of course she didn't mean that, and I know I'm worth more than my maid services. I just forget it sometimes when it seems that's all I get done in a day and when I resent the never-ending duties of living.

Sometimes I stand barefoot in my kitchen only because we have to eat, no one else is home to cook, and I don't feel like wearing shoes. But other times I enjoy making food for the people I love and I like to feel the holy ground of my home.

On the days I touch holiness, I am thankful to have this home and family where I give and receive love and where I have no trouble knowing that I, too, am holy. That reminder transforms everything I am and do.

**Think of the ground,
where you stand and walk today, as holy.**

Remove the sandals from your feet,
for the place where you stand is holy.

—Joshua 5:15

Support System

A long article appeared in the Sunday newspaper about a mother who was arrested for trying to sell her babies. The oldest was nine months, the youngest still *in utero*. The story was written to incite the readers' anger toward the woman; it never acknowledged the part of ourselves that sometimes feels overwhelmed with the task of mothering.

The article went on to say what anyone could have guessed. She was young, poor, without family support, and had few friends beyond a husband who was a substance abuser.

A good support system makes all the difference as to which side of that fine line I fall, between being overwhelmed or empowered. When I feel support, I tend to take it for granted. I wonder if that's why God sent the shepherds to the holy family who was on the road away from their support system!

**Thank God for each system
that supports your motherhood.**

So they went with haste
and found Mary and Joseph,
and the child lying in the manger.

—Luke 2:16

Nurturing Oneself

This morning I paid someone to take care of my baby. I went to the coffee shop, ordered a decadent pastry, and watched the clouds. It's been a long time since I looked at the clouds. It's been a long time since I spent time, all alone, doing nothing.

I felt bad at first for leaving the baby, for spending the money, and for eating empty calories. But then I felt my body relax. My shoulders came down from their height where they were poised for action. My legs stretched out where I knew they could stay for a while. My head began to empty itself. God's presence filled my whole being.

I returned home, refreshed. I resolved not to wait so long to nurture myself again.

**What would you tell a friend
under stress to do for herself?
Do it for yourself.**

I will give thanks to the Lord
with my whole heart.

—Psalm 111:1

God's Image

Today I sat in a room full of people. Many variations of wealth, status, and personality were represented. Suddenly I thought about the origin of each one of us. At one time we were each a tiny dot, developing in the wombs of our mothers. We were all birthed and remained dependent on others for many months.

What a transformation of that group! We were all reduced, or maybe elevated, to equality in the sight of our Creator. I laughed. Motherhood has surely had an impact on how I see the world!

**You have something in common
with every other mother in the history
of the world. You are a co-creator with God.**

My soul magnifies the Lord.

—Luke 1:46

Illness

"How would you feel about the four of us praying together right now for your baby?" The question from my pastor pulled dissonant strings on my inner chords.

First I felt ashamed that I had spent the past half hour complaining to him and his wife about our battle with weeks of colds and ear infections, without my even thinking about prayer. My embarrassment quickly blended into relief, however, that he had thought of it and offered it to us. It was active proof that I was not alone. My silent, lonely prayers in the dark were enhanced through the strength of our numbers.

I finally relaxed in their support. Our baby wasn't healed instantly, but I was.

**Let one or two others
know how they can give you their prayers.**

"Peace, peace to the far and to the near,"
says the Lord, "and I will heal them."

—Isaiah 57:19

Stability

For the first thirty years of my life, I despised the thought of stability. Life was too short to be anything less than impulsive. There were too many good people to meet and fun places to live to stay in the same spot for long.

Suddenly, however, stability doesn't seem so bad. As flexible as I know children can be, I long to provide as much solid ground for my baby as possible. I can feel my roots starting to sink in to daily routines, neighborhood comforts, my church family. I'm keeping photo albums updated with pictures of distant friends and relatives. Surprisingly enough, it actually feels good!

**Even in change,
a mother's consistent love
will provide stability for her child.**

And now faith, hope, and love abide,
these three; and the greatest of these is love.
—I Corinthians 13:13

Self-Reliance

Last night I went out for dessert with a bunch of other mothers. I don't know which was the best treat—eating the double-decker fudge sundae that I didn't make or have to clean up, or hearing all of my struggles and joys mirrored in the experiences of my friends. The camaraderie was comforting and energizing.

It's inevitable, however, that I'm alone again today. I may share similar situations with others, but the results of my decisions and actions are still my own. Both are more and more important—my community, as well as my sense of self-reliance.

**I'm grateful, O God,
for how you come to me,
through others and within myself.**

Let everything that breathes praise the Lord.

—Psalm 150:6

Exhaustion

We had guests stay with us over the weekend. By 9 p.m. Monday we were wondering why we were so tired. After all, we didn't do much with them except sit around watching the baby and eat.

We aren't used to staying up until midnight anymore, and our childless guests had no reason to think of anything different. Of course they weren't the ones getting up again at 6 a.m. It does take a lot of energy to have food and drinks ever-available for two extra people and to keep the house relatively tidy.

Part of taking care of myself is knowing what I need. The other part is letting others know.

**Your needs have changed,
so don't forget to change your
expectations of yourself as well.**

I will satisfy the weary,
and all who are faint I will replenish.
—Jeremiah 31:25

211

Mystery

I often wonder what's going on in her little head. Those deep brown eyes are strong communicators, but I can't grasp what all they're saying. Sometimes she looks at me as if she can see inside me, but I can't see inside her. I get many clues about who she is, but I will never know her fully.

I cannot determine happiness for my daughter. Nor can I dictate her spirituality or personality. I can only walk beside her. There's something scary about that, but also some relief.

**Enjoy the mystery that lives
so close but cannot be owned by you.**

Think of us this way,
as servants of Christ and stewards of God's mysteries.
—I Corinthians 4:1

Death

ast week my cousin, a year older than I, died of cancer. I hadn't known her in recent years, so her absence won't affect my daily routine, but I couldn't stop sobbing at her funeral. When I saw her husband holding their eleven-month-old son, I knew where my tears came from. They were for myself, for my own life.

I've wondered before how I could bear to lose a parent or how I could go on living without my husband. I thought I would rather die myself than be left alone, but now that I have a child, I can't imagine my own death. I want to nurture my daughter and watch her grow. I want to be her stability. I know others love her, too, but right now I desperately want to be the most important person in her life.

Peace to mothers who are dying
and to my fear of death.

Blessed are those who mourn,
for they will be comforted.

—Matthew 5:4

Enjoying the Present

I often find myself trying to explain things to my baby. He gurgles. I tell him what I'm thinking. He smiles. I can't wait to hear what that little brain is thinking and dreaming. His clear blue eyes look at me, full of mystery.

I wonder if, when he's old enough for us to talk and understand each other, I'll long for these days of simplicity and unspoken wonder. Just in case, I think I'll concentrate on enjoying this stage as much as possible today.

**Close your eyes and imagine a seed of love,
growing from deep within you and spreading
over your body. When it gets so big it opens
your eyes and ears and mouth,
let it spread all over your baby.**

Awake, O north wind,
and come, O south wind!
Blow upon my garden
that its fragrance may be wafted abroad.
—Song of Solomon 4:16

Anti-Cuddly

I am starting to come to terms with the fact that, much to my dismay, I do not have a cuddle-bunny. I always thought cuddly and baby were synonymous, but this child obviously doesn't agree with that. Is she really a baby if she's not cuddly?

I wanted to nurse her for a year, but she couldn't tolerate looking at nothing but me. She wanted the independence offered by a bottle. I try to comfort her when she falls over and she pushes me away, eager to try again.

I asked a friend what I'm doing wrong and she said, "Some babies are just like that." I guess I'm not always in a cuddly mood either, as God especially knows.

**Help me, Lord,
to recognize and accept the unique personality
of my daughter.**

His mother treasured
all these things in her heart.

—Luke 2:51

215

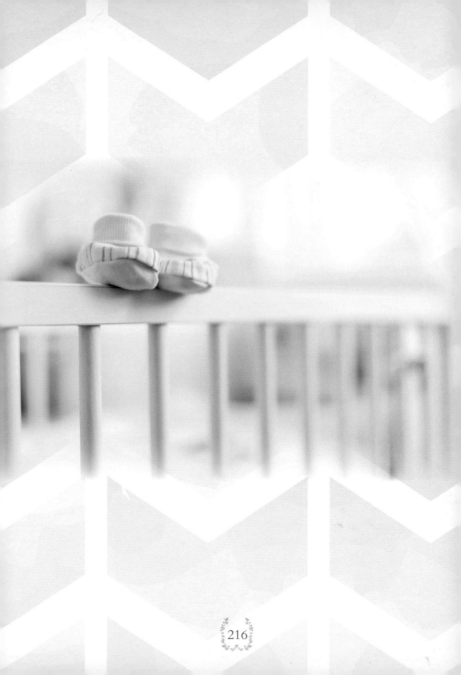

Energy

I'm too old for this. After doing thirty deep knee-bends while carrying twenty extra pounds, my joints ache. By ten o'clock at night when I'm washing what appears to be a week's worth of dishes, I notice a tight pain across my back. I get done playing on the floor long before my son does. He's a study in constant motion and I yearn for an elusive moment of calm.

Come to think of it, though, babies sometimes wore me out when I was a teenager, too. And some days now, being with my baby puts new life in my bones. The intermingling of energies is the gift for which I remain grateful.

**Imagine the energy of your baby,
dancing its way into your body.**

You have turned
my mourning into dancing.

—Psalm 30:11

Transformation

I kept waiting to return to normal. And normal, of course, meant being who I was before I had a baby.

I'm slowly beginning to believe, however, that as in all of life, there is no going back. Living means changing, and I have taken on one of the greatest possibilities for change by assuming responsibility for another life!

Maybe if I think of this process as a transformation, I will experience it as an enchanted diversion, filling me with wonder, rather than a dreaded mutation, restricting my potential. I'll bet caterpillars don't always like the cocoon stage either.

**Look for the part of your life
where wings have developed
because you have a baby.**

There are many who say,
"O that we might see some good!"
—Psalm 4:6

Advice

I spent time with a friend today who has a younger baby than mine. I felt strange to be answering her questions about babies. I've been the one asking them of everyone else for so long.

But I also liked it! I realized that I do know some things about being a mother. At least I know what's working for my baby and me. The hard part will be letting go of my advice now, and letting my friend figure out what's best for her baby and her!

**Advice can be wonderful
as long as it's not a cover for control.**

Those who know your name
put their trust in you, for you,
O Lord, have not forsaken those who seek you.
—Psalm 9:10

Lack of Sleep

I fought to escape the fog of my short night when I heard my husband at the bedroom door saying, "There's Mommy. Wanna go to Mommy?"

"No!" I yelled. "I hate that." I knew he would plop Jonathan on me and go back to his breakfast, and Jonathan would squirm and cry until I woke up enough to feed him. I'd rather get up alone and at least splash some water on my face before I face the relentless motion of the day.

I wish I would make myself get up before Jonathan, so I could get myself together before motherhood attacks. But I'm so tired . . . oops, I must have fallen back to sleep!

**Lack of sleep is a fact of motherhood.
The sooner I accept it, the less energy
I'll lose trying to change it.**

O Lord,
in the morning you hear my voice.

—Psalm 5:3

Act of Love

One of my friends told me she's leaving her husband because she's not attracted to him anymore. She doesn't hate him, but she doesn't like him either.

It scares me as I think about my own marriage. We get angry at each other and we don't always like each other. I know I haven't been the easiest person to live with, especially this past year with all the ups and downs of adjusting to life with a baby.

Watching how we relate to our baby, however, might help steady our marriage. I don't like to get up in the middle of the night to a screaming infant. I don't enjoy changing sheets after she throws up on them. I'm not attracted to the smell of dirty diapers. But she's my baby and I've committed myself to raising her, whether every minute is lovely or not. My love for her grows by doing acts of love. My love for my husband will also grow by doing acts of love, even when I don't like him.

Plan an act of love for your lover.

This is my beloved and this is my friend.
—Song of Solomon 5:16

Resentment

Now that we have a baby, I look at other childless couples as single and independent. We were single together for the first years of our marriage, and even though we often chose to spend our free time together, we also had different interests that we could pursue with limited disruption to the other's life.

Now, however, I make few choices without them affecting at least one other person, or two—my baby and my husband. I also catch myself keeping track of how many times I've made supper or washed dishes in a row, and resentment builds when I deem my load unfair. Blanket statements have increased, like "I always . . ." or "You never . . ."

Our lives are more interconnected than ever. To keep resentment controlled—and our home and our nerves in some harmony—we need to give concentrated effort to our communication skills.

Where is the resentment in your life?
Take one step to resolve it.

Keep your heart with all vigilance,
for from it flow the springs of life.

—Proverbs 4:23

Mothering Job

My husband and I have finally figured out how we can make my job of mothering seem as worthwhile as a full-time job that earns money. We've set up a budget with an allowance for me to use without accountability. It's a concrete way to remind me that, even though I'm earning less money than my husband right now, my time with our baby is just as valuable.

I hate that I don't always know that. I wish my head, which knows the importance of mothering, would dominate my feelings. Too often I listen to the attitude that devalues its importance. Earning money isn't the indicator that tells me how valuable I am, so why do I act like it is?

In the meantime, I hope the allowance idea works. We're both working hard for this money.

**Are your attitudes toward your job
of mothering the ones you believe in?**

More to be desired are they [the ordinances of the Lord]
than gold, even much fine gold.

—Psalm 19:10

Quiet

I finished work early today and, instead of picking Maria up then, I went home to be alone. The familiar house seemed strange. There were no voices, no music, not even the anticipation of noise to which I would need to respond. The toys, strewn as I had left them, were full of silence and immobility.

So many possibilities lay within this hour for myself. I sat down on the couch to rest my feet and decide what to do first. I let my head muscles sink into a cushion—another unfamiliar luxury.

An hour later I awoke, just in time to go get Maria. That was an hour well spent!

**If quiet time alone is a relative
once removed, schedule a visit.**

In righteousness you shall be established.
—Isaiah 54:14

Production-Oriented

I'm still too production-oriented for the good of my life as a mother. Last night I apologized for not having a reason for going to bed early. It had been one of those days when, no matter how liberated I like to think I am from traditional male/female roles, I needed a wife. I didn't get the wash hung up until three in the afternoon. I couldn't think of anything to make for lunch or supper. I didn't send my brother's birthday card, and I didn't make any of the phone calls on my list.

Fortunately my husband is sometimes better at recognizing the stress of motherhood than I am. He noticed the toys with which we had played, the books we had read, the groceries we had bought, and the contentedness of a baby who had been well cared for and loved all day. He said he knew exactly why I was so tired. I slept better, having a reason.

Cultivate internal credit.
External credit may not always be forthcoming.

Whoever gives even a cup of cold water
to one of these little ones in the name of a disciple—
truly I tell you, none of these will lose their reward.
—Matthew 10:42

Love

When we first talked about whether or not to have a child, my husband wondered if he would have the time and energy for another primary relationship. He is an introvert, and living with me takes enough of his energy so that he periodically needs time alone to be renewed.

I am an extrovert who gets my energy from others. I wasn't sure how I'd fit a baby in time-wise, but I knew a child would certainly add another flavor to the party of life! Babies were something we hadn't tried yet, but others seemed to be enjoying them, so why not us?

What we have both learned is that love doesn't divide. It only multiplies. This child has received more love from us than we knew we had to give, and it has put more love into our lives than we knew existed.

**Thank you, God,
for letting us experience the multiplication table of love.**

God's love has been poured into our hearts
through the Holy Spirit that has been given to us.
—Romans 5:5

Anger

I got so angry at my child today that it scared me! I was tired and she wouldn't take her nap. So I decided to go for a drive and let the car motion lull her to sleep. When I tried to put her in her car seat, she stiffened up and I couldn't do anything. I thought I was supposed to be the adult making the decisions, and I had lost control to this baby!

I finally brought her back to the house, put her in the crib, went to the other end of the house so I wouldn't hear her crying, and called a friend. I didn't know a baby could be so stubborn, and I didn't know I could be so furious!

I'm not proud of letting myself explode. I am proud of myself, however, that I didn't hurt her, because now I know I could have. Child abuse is no longer unfathomable. It's still unacceptable, but I understand how a tired, stressed parent with few resources could let it happen.

God,
protect this child and me from each other.

In your anger do not sin.

—Psalm 4:4

Anger

When I was angry yesterday and called my friend, I blurted out all the awful feelings that were exploding in me. Somewhere I had gotten the idea that good mothers don't get angry with their children, especially their babies. But I was too desperate to hold it in.

I think I expected my friend to give me some advice or refer me to a psychiatrist, because I was shocked when I heard her understanding laugh. "You sound like a real mother now," she said. Somehow the permission to be angry at my own child freed me to give up the anger—and the guilt. There are some people with whom I wouldn't share my dark side, but what a relief to have some friends who can hear it without thinking I'm an awful mother.

**God, too,
can hear your anger.**

Even with me the Lord was angry.
—Deuteronomy 1:37

Prayer

This morning I listened to another mother talk about her daily hour of prayer. She encouraged me to keep my relationship with God a priority. I suddenly felt a longing for that familiar quiet time. It's been so long since I enjoyed that luxury—before the baby, in fact!

I have to believe, though, that holding my child is prayer. Dressing her, making her comfortable, rocking her, showing the world to her—these are all extensions of God parenting me, of our relationship of prayer.

I don't get up with her in the middle of the night because I love it. God has graced me with a capacity to nurture that goes beyond my human desires. That, too, is prayer.

This mothering prayer is not yet familiar. I guess, though, that I have plenty of time to learn.

Recognize how pervasive your relationship is with God, in every aspect of motherhood. Call it prayer.

Pray in the Spirit
at all times in every prayer and supplication.
—Ephesians 6:18

Marriage

After the baby was finally asleep last night, I looked at my husband. He was wrapped in a blanket on the rocker, watching TV. I suddenly realized how little I have been a wife. I've been so busy at this mothering thing that I've been neglecting my part in our marriage.

During supper conversations I give a rendition of all the cute things the baby does, or what he does that worries me. We've made meals, washed clothes, and done many of the tasks of marriage together. But we haven't told each other about ourselves for days!

So I asked if I could share his blanket. I asked him how his day had been and he asked about mine. It felt wonderful to be a wife again.

**Marriage preceded your role as parent.
Find a way to nurture yours today
so it will outlast parenthood as well.**

A man leaves his father and his mother
and clings to his wife and they become one flesh.
—Genesis 2:24

Change

Carmen and I thought we would find a babysitter, go out in the world, and act like the old friends we used to be before we had children. We had lunch—just the two of us—and I discreetly refrained from reaching over to mash her peaches. Then we had fun shopping. It's true we did buy some toys, but we also each bought a shirt for ourselves.

We were proud of that single, independent feeling we could recall on demand, until she went to sign a check. All she could find was a broken crayon. And when I reached in my pocket to help her, I pulled out a pacifier. Seems like we can never again not be mothers!

**God,
I love your sense of humor!**

For everything there is a season.
—Ecclesiastes 3:1

Home

Maria was born a week earlier than we expected, and it's not an exaggeration to say that I was not at all ready. We were just beginning a series of prepared child-birth classes, I hadn't packed a hospital bag, baby clothes that were given to us were in their packages rather than washed with baby detergent, and our study was still occupying the room we intended for the nursery. I guess I was going to do all that the day before her due date. I don't remember.

I do remember that it didn't seem to matter to her. Love welcomed her into the world and that was the main thing she needed.

Help me to focus, Lord,
on what I have instead of what I don't have.

There was no place for them in the inn.
—Luke 2:7

Adult Childhood

I could hardly believe it when my husband came back from a trip to the toy store with a set of blocks for our baby, who was barely able to hold a block in her hand. He gleefully sat down, dumped the blocks out in the middle of the living room, and chattered happily to his daughter as "they" built a castle. Her part was to sit there and watch.

I wondered if these were blocks like he had when he was a boy, or maybe wished he had. I had never seen this side of his creativity before. Maybe he's been needing an excuse to buy some blocks for a long time.

I like seeing the resurrected little boy in him.

**Take the help
your child gives you to relive your own childhood.**

The child grew and became strong,
filled with wisdom;
and the favor of God was upon him.

—Luke 2:40

Wholeness

Actions speak louder than words. That's what I've heard. When I think about my baby learning more from me by watching than by what I say, I realize the many dimensions of that fact.

Yes, I'm still responsible and happy to care for her, but when I think of teaching her self-sufficiency, it isn't by doing everything for her. To teach her trust, I need to trust her, too, with as much as each progressive age can handle. If I take time to nurture myself, physically, emotionally, socially, mentally, and spiritually, she will learn how to be independent. When I go to others for support, she will learn interdependence. As I meet my own needs, my daughter will learn how to meet her needs, too. She will learn to love herself in a healthy way as she observes me loving myself.

**Look in the mirror of your child's behavior
and words to get some sense of whether
or not you are who you want to be.**

Let the peoples renew their strength:
let them approach, then let them speak;
let us together draw near for judgment.

—Isaiah 41:1

Angels

I can already tell that "You make me nervous!" is going to be a permanent phrase in my vocabulary. My son is not even walking, yet he has an uncanny knack for putting his life in constant danger.

Today he pulled a lamp down on himself. Last week his exploring fingers told me to get those outlet covers on, now! And of course, he's rolled off the bed twice in his short life. His speed makes me feel like I move in slow motion. I don't think anyone can be a mother very long without believing in guardian angels.

**God,
I'll take as many extra angels
as you can spare for this son of mine.**

For he will command his angels
concerning you to guard you in all your ways.
—Psalm 91:11

Reflection

My husband had been sitting in the kitchen for an hour, doing nothing that I could see except pulling out his tape measure occasionally. He had said he was planning to work tonight so I finally asked him what he was doing.

"Looking and thinking," he said. I teased him that it takes him as long to think about something as to do it. Instead of feeling teased, he thought I finally understood!

Maybe that's why when he does something, it's done well. I can go and go all day without really taking time to look and think. When I schedule time to reflect, however, I am a better mother.

Is it time to stop doing and just be?

My soul waits for the Lord more than
those who watch for the morning.
—Psalm 130:6

Simple Creativity

I finally figured I'm never going to fulfill my wish to be creative as long as I just sit around waiting for the big explosion. So I decided to add a creative touch to all the things I needed to do today.

First I sneaked a love note into John's lunch bag. I glued a dried flower to the notebook paper on which I was writing to my parents. I floated a sprig of mint in my iced tea. I put a familiar rice and beans meal on a special platter for supper and plopped some parsley in the middle. It wasn't much, but it changed my day.

Anyone who finds joy in a baby's first smile, the new contortion of his face, or the muscles that have built up enough to roll his body over, can find creativity in the simple pleasures of a day.

Simple pleasures are easier to come by than waiting for a big one.

The Lord is my shepherd;
I shall not want.

—Psalm 23:1

Encouragement

I've been told that I should expect affirmation least from those persons who are in the same line of work as I am. Silent competition apparently wins out over unguarded encouragement, even with friends.

I realized today that the job of mothering is sadly no different. One of my friends told me she thinks I'm a good mother. The warm tingles that crept all over my body and bathed my soul told me that I don't hear that much. I don't think I've said it to anyone else recently either!

Which friend comes to mind
when you think of a good mother? Tell her.

I want their hearts to be encouraged and united in love.
—Colossians 2:2

Laughter

I had a wonderful evening. Some friends were here for supper and it was an ordinary time together, except that we laughed a lot.

I still don't feel real smooth entertaining with a growing infant whose constant demands make it impossible to complete any conversation. Our guests' child, a little older, added to the confusion, too, but they had already found a remedy. Instead of letting the frustration build so we could all know the evening was a flop, they laughed.

They laughed when the prayer was interrupted by the babies having a shouting match. They laughed as we shared all the mundane inconveniences babies bring to our lives. They laughed when the good smells of our anticipated dessert were ruined by the bad smells babies invariably produce after dinner. They were a refreshing change from the times I've worried about everything being exactly right.

A few problems are real. The rest can be laughed away.

He who sits in the heavens laughs.

—Psalm 2:4

242

Beauty

"Weren't the clouds beautiful today?" John asked when he came home from work. I didn't have a response, because the embarrassing truth is, I didn't look at the sky all day. I had been outside several times. I even took a long walk, but, no, I definitely did not see the clouds.

When I walk these days, I'm watching the stroller to make sure the baby stays in it, or just to enjoy how cute he is. I'm looking for bumps so I can ease the shock and for puddles to miss. When I drive I'm playing baby music, handing out toys and snacks, and wishing we were at our destination. I rarely just sit and look out the window.

I'm glad the clouds were beautiful today. I'm glad, too, for all the other beauty I was watching instead.

**Focus on the added beauty in your life,
instead of feeling bad about what you're missing.**

The heavens are telling the glory of God.
—Psalm 19:1

Adaptability

"Do you need to go?

I didn't understand the question until I realized that my caller was hearing my baby crying. "No, we're fine," I answered as I readjusted the phone between my ear and shoulder, turned the stove down, and finished changing a diaper.

I must finally be adapting! I used to save all my phone calls, heavy conversations, and thinking for after the baby was in bed. But I was always too tired to do any of that by then. Somewhere along the line, I started juggling. Now I'm beginning to realize that the balls are no longer flying in all different directions! I still drop some, but I catch a few, too.

**Thank you, God,
that new skills have come with new responsibilities.**

My help comes from the Lord
who made heaven and earth.

—Psalm 121:2

Live the Questions

There's something in me that yearns for answers. When I enter a new stage with my baby, I poll everyone I see to find out what they think I should be doing. I want to know how I'm supposed to act and feel and what to do if I don't get it right.

Yet I hear a voice reminding me, "Watch out for the boredom of answers and the trickery that makes you think you've got everything under control." Living in the questions reminds me of this baby's—and my own—uniqueness.

**Understand your questions
as the creative tension that gives energy to your life.**

Satisfy us in the morning with your steadfast love,
so that we may rejoice and be glad all our days.
—Psalm 90:14

Love

"Love outweighs a multitude of wrong actions or words." I don't remember where I first heard that, but the truth of it comes to me now as comfort. I wanted desperately to be a perfect mom, but it didn't take long to see I wouldn't be able to live up to that, no matter how hard I tried.

I still believe I can be a good mom most of the time, though. I'm also confident that the insurance in which I've invested will cover me the rest of the time—love insurance.

**God,
continue to multiply my love,
as well as others' love for me.**

The one who loves has fulfilled the law.

—Romans 13:8

Ungrateful

I just figured out why changing diapers is such a pain. It's not the mess or the smell or the time involved that bothers me the most. It's the ungratefulness!

I can't tell that my baby appreciates my efforts at all. She usually screams when I lay her down on her back, and then clings to me like I'm going to torture her if she lets go! Her struggling makes the task take twice as long as it would if she were relaxed.

One would think the first words my child would learn would be "thank you" for all she's been given. But then, look at her role model. "Thank you" is not usually the first phrase out of my mouth either!

**Be consciously grateful
for a few of the comfort measures
you're enjoying at this moment.**

I will give to the Lord
the thanks due to his righteousness.

—Psalm 7:17

Change

I always thought I'd be one of those people who could have a baby without letting it affect the activity of my life too much. I'd take him along to my meetings. He could watch me put on clown makeup and be part of the act. I'd already bought a bicycle seat so he could train right along with me; someone would bring him to my races so he could welcome me across the finish line.

But sometimes he wants his own bed before my meetings are over. My clown face scares him, and riding on the back of my bicycle doesn't begin to satisfy his need for exercise.

I could make him fit into my schedule as planned. But the force of my desire for his well-being has caught me off guard. It's taking over my interest in continuing my activities without adjustment.

Step boldly into the new.

New things I now declare.

—Isaiah 42:9

249

Blessed Hands

I read a poem this week that started each line with, "Blessed be these hands . . ." Since then I've been noticing where my hands go and what they do. They have hugged, carried, and cuddled. They've washed dishes, faces, and bottoms. They've dug in the soil and created meals. They've scrubbed and caressed. They've kneaded bread and hit computer keys. They've picked up toys, turned pages, and tucked a baby into bed.

My hands do more than I usually think about. And every encounter, now that I pay attention, has been most blessed.

**Look at your hands,
thanking God for everything they have done
in the last twenty-four hours.**

Whatever your hand finds to do,
do with your might.

—Ecclesiastes 9:10

Helping Others

I told a friend who has just become a mother that I'd bring supper over for them tonight. So when my baby went to sleep, I hurried to the kitchen to produce a meal. As I prepared the menu, I remembered how much I appreciated all the meals brought to us when I was first home from the hospital. I prayed for my friend and her new family as I chopped, blended, and baked.

I thoroughly enjoyed finally packing the food into containers that would hold the heat until it reached her table. It's wonderful to be switching to the giving end of this social grace.

**Thank you, God,
for the gradual, but sure,
return of energy.**

She opens her hand to the poor
and reaches out her hands to the needy.
—Proverbs 31:20

Abnormal Babies

The doctors had told us, after looking at my blood work, that our baby might be born with a birth defect. The chances were very slight, but we should prepare ourselves.

Our accompanying fear was not so slight, though. Sometimes we could rationalize or pray the fear away, but it always sneaked back.

Now it is obvious that our baby is developing healthily and I am relieved. I rarely remember those early fears. Every once in a while, however, I think of those who have birthed babies in that one percent chance we missed; the ones whose joy in giving birth has needed to change to allow for a different future than they had planned. Today my relief is tempered by the pain of those mothers.

**God,
help me to experience my joy fully
without blocking my awareness of the pain around me.**

Your eyes beheld my unformed substance.

—Psalm 139:16

Growing

Sometimes I feel as though I'm finally catching on to how to be a mother. I have a routine for my days now, so they don't feel so chaotic—at least not all the time. The joy of being with my baby is growing. Even the worries and fears about all I don't know are under control.

That is *sometimes*. Today I caught my baby eating the dirt from an overturned flowerpot. I know I left him playing on the other side of the room only a minute before! My mastery of the infancy stage is already outdated. I better put the plants up higher while I figure out how to do this next chapter.

**In the scramble to stay ahead of your child,
give yourself credit for all you are learning.**

The child grew and became strong in spirit.
—Luke 1:80

Miracle Babies

Every time a baby is born at the treatment center for recovering addicts where I work, we take a picture of the infant and put it on our bulletin board under the heading, "Our Miracle Babies." Conceived in a body that's also ingesting drugs, each baby born there is certainly a miracle.

Even though I didn't use drugs, my baby feels like no less of a miracle. I know I couldn't have created this intricate being, nor have I done anything to deserve the gift of her life in mine. The greatness of God is not only something I will pass on to my child. It is also what my child is passing on to me.

See the miracle anew today.

One generation shall laud your works to another
and shall declare your mighty acts.

—Psalm 145:4

Balancing Work and Home

I'm trying to figure out how to balance being home with my baby and working to provide for his needs. I don't have a choice about some of the monthly bills—they have to be paid so we have a place to live and food to eat. But beyond that, how much more do I need to earn for leisure activities, educational opportunities, a bigger house, toys and books, clothes, and eating out?

I want to be a good provider, and some extras are nice, but how many extras are worth my being away from home to make them possible? I have a feeling this is one dilemma for which the baby books or friends won't provide my answers. I also have a feeling it's a question I won't be able to answer once and for all.

God, give me your wisdom.

Wisdom will come into your heart,
and knowledge will be pleasant to your soul.
—Proverbs 2:10

Failed Attempts

One of the ways I thought I might solve yesterday's dilemma, between trying to balance earning money and being with my child, was to work at home. I know lots of mothers who take care of other people's children in their homes as a way of doing both. So I offered to watch a friend's baby for one afternoon a week as an experiment.

Well, it may look ideal when other people do it, but it took me one afternoon to question whether it would work for me, and two to terminate those efforts!

I felt terrible when both babies needed my attention. I felt bad if I didn't pick up the baby I was being paid to watch, yet my heart broke to not hold my own when he needed me. My arms nearly collapsed when I held them both!

This solution may work for some, but I'll have to find another one.

**Accept your limitations
and accent your strengths.**

The Lord upholds all who are falling,
and raises up all who are bowed down.

—Psalm 145:14

Good Days

Today I feel invincible. I'm a good mother with a beautiful baby and no one's advice is going to invade my good sense. I will smile graciously at unsolicited remarks and go on my merry way. My baby's crying is even precious today!

Why am I always trying to figure out what's wrong with me on bad days, but I have no interest in analysis on a day like this? But who cares? I don't have time to work at that today. The world is too lovely.

**Thank you, God,
for the gift of joy.**

Clap your hands,
all you peoples;
shout to God with loud songs of joy.

—Psalm 47:1

Marriage and Parenthood

Kisses when we part have been kept alive in our marriage by an old family saying: "Those who kiss their spouses good-bye have fewer accidents!" We haven't needed a motto to remind us to give kisses of greeting. They happen automatically because we've missed each other.

I wondered what a baby would do to the primacy of our love for each other as husband and wife. As our baby has become more responsive, I expected John to be drawn to her first when he comes home from work. No matter how adorable she is, though, he still kisses me first and I love it! Someday when she has grown secure in the love her parents have for each other, I think she'll understand and appreciate its strength.

Let your husband know your love.

Set me as a seal upon your heart.
—Song of Solomon 8:6

Messy?

"This is one part of having kids I couldn't deal with!" I looked to see where my friend's eyes were focused. It was the first time Sally had been over for lunch since her wedding, and she had unfortunately been seated beside the baby.

Sally was repulsed by what I saw as delightful—the baby's efforts to bend his fingers in just the right way to grab his food and move it toward his mouth. I saw how much he actually got in; she saw how much remained on his face, in his hair, on the floor, and, worst of all, in her lap. Poor Sally. She loves children, but I guess she'll have to be a mother before she recognizes this as progress.

**Appreciate how much your baby
has helped change your vision.**

Wisdom is at home in the mind
of one who has understanding.

—Proverbs 14:33

Change

"Baby" and "change" are nearly synonymous. I no sooner figure out her rhythms than she changes them. I don't know when to fill in the part in her baby book that says, "Baby's Daily Routine." We've had so many!

As far as I can tell, this baby seems to eagerly greet change. Change is her invitation to life, and she moves ahead by accepting it. Yes, she seems to embrace it.

I have a harder time welcoming change. It feels more like disruption, intrusion designed to alienate me from life. Maybe watching my baby blossom with change will help me let it into my life more gracefully.

**Is change
your companion or adversary?**

We will not all die,
but we will all be changed.
—I Corinthians 15:51

Stability

I feel incredibly settled! What a novel word to use to describe myself. I haven't decided if I like it or not.

When I was twenty-four years old, I quit my job to go on vacation and got another one when I got back. I moved every year or two, enjoying lots of different places and people. I explored at least ten thousand miles of the country by bicycle.

Suddenly, however, "settled" is not such a bad word. A steady job, lasting friends, and a stable home are growing in importance to me. Riding my bike across town is far enough. Stability, for now, is a gift I can offer my child.

**God,
for the days I can receive the changes
I'm making without resentment,
I give you thanks.**

The Lord is exalted . . .
he will be the stability of your times.
—Isaiah 33:5, 6

Reading

At first I felt a little foolish reading aloud to the baby when she obviously couldn't understand a word I was saying. But all my friends who are early childhood educators say they can tell which children have been read to at home and no one knows how early they benefit from it. At the very least, babies like to hear the rhythm of words while being held. Books, designs, and colors stimulate their imaginations.

I admit I rather enjoy the colors and simple profundity of some of these children's books myself! The challenge will be to enjoy the repetition as much as my child does.

**Read to your baby today,
no matter the age.**

Truly I tell you,
unless you change and become like children,
you will never enter the kingdom of heaven.
—Matthew 18:3

Time-Out

It sounds, from the books, like this little innocent baby will soon be asserting himself and trying to find where the boundaries are. So I've been reading about different theories of discipline. Giving a child a brief time-out, in order to interrupt its concentration on something destructive, makes sense to me.

I haven't found anything written about *my* time-outs, though. That's hardly fair. I've already discovered my need of them. Sometimes just removing myself from a frustrating situation and counting to ten does a lot to give me a new way of seeing things.

**God,
help me remember to break
my moments of tumult with time-outs.**

Let your good spirit lead me on a level path.
—Psalm 143:10

Anger

I'm so angry tonight. After I finally got the baby to bed, there were still dishes to do, laundry to put away, and cookies to finish baking. And John was sitting on the couch watching some dumb TV show. I know that's what he needs to unwind from his day, and I know he probably would have helped me if I would have asked him to, but I wanted him to see the work himself. I want him to read my mind so I don't have to feel like a nag.

I try not to keep track of who does the most housework, but it's hard not to on a night like this. Life is just not fair.

**God,
thank you for listening to my anger.**

You gave me room when I was in distress.
Be gracious to me, and hear my prayer.

—Psalm 4:1

Anger Revisited

It was helpful to spout off my anger on paper last night. I unloaded some of it that way. I got rid of the rest of it when I finished the jobs I was working on and went to bed, while John stayed up to finish some work on the trim in the bathroom remodeling project. I guess we just see different things to do and have a different sense of timing about when to do them.

I still think it's okay to be angry and to express it. I'm glad, though, that this time I expressed my anger on paper first. That helped me to put it in perspective and to deal with my feelings without involving John's feelings.

**Thank you, God,
for helping me gain perspective on my anger.**

You have put gladness in my heart.

—Psalm 4:7

On Being Late

I hate being late. But what else can I do when the baby has a major blowout as we're heading out the door? Any decent mother would be late because of a diaper change, right?

If anyone is five minutes late for a meeting with four other people, I figure they've wasted twenty minutes of other people's time, five minutes that belonged to each of the four members. But what can I do when the babysitter's late or, worse yet, forgets to come? Suddenly I'm the "they" I always thought was so inconsiderate.

Maybe this is another one of those growing edges brought to me, courtesy of motherhood. I'm being forced to quit being judgmental of others and to plan generously for the extra preparation time my own baby takes. Maybe occasionally I'll just have to forgive others, as well as myself.

Are you your own worst critic?

You bless the righteous, O Lord;
you cover them with favor as with a shield.

—Psalm 5:12

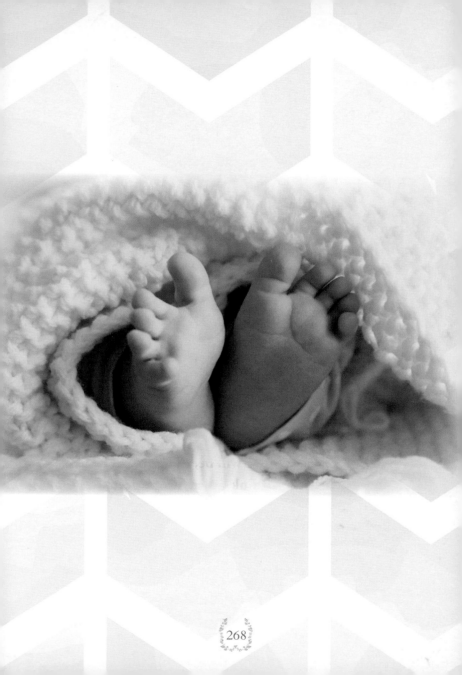

Housework

Ihung up the phone, delighted that an old friend was coming to visit and meet the baby. Then I turned to face a disaster. Before the phone rang I was playing contentedly with my baby in what I now perceived as a horrible mess!

After a frantic, impulsive attempt to look presentable, I stopped to look at my options. Housework just isn't a critically important thing to me anymore. In fact, my ego will not be crushed if my friend thinks I've turned into a slob.

I returned to playing with my baby while I waited for my friend to arrive. That was more fun for both of us.

**God,
thank you for the days I have enough
strength to decide who I will be, rather than simply
react to what I think others will expect.**

This is the day that the Lord has made;
let us rejoice and be glad in it.

—Psalm 118:24

Passion

I had a wonderful time planning a tea party this week. I invited all the mothers I knew would be free in the middle of the week. We talked, shared tea and cake, watched our babies crawl all over each other, and took turns jumping up when one of them moved out of reach.

After they left, I felt a deep satisfaction. I had provided a space and atmosphere to share what we usually each do in our own separate homes—watch our babies. I had offered a celebration, for no particular reason. It was especially fun to feel a passion for something—even as simple as organizing and preparing a tea party. Passion motivates me and leaves me feeling satisfied.

Thank you, God, for giving me passion and helping me to find expression for it.

> Love is strong as death,
> passion fierce as the grave.
> —Song of Solomon 8:6

Bulldozer

I was a bulldozer today. I was single-minded in my goal to get ready for our weekend trip. I had no time for the neighbor who wanted to chat. Maria wouldn't go to sleep on my schedule, so I mowed the lawn with one hand while I held her in the other. Later, my arm became numb and I put her into the backpack. That's where she fell asleep while I washed the dishes. I let the answering machine screen my phone calls, and I almost literally mowed down the old lady blocking "my" aisle at the grocery store.

Looking back, being a bulldozer was not a pleasant experience for any of us who were involved. The challenge remains: how to be as efficient as possible without being obnoxious.

**Invite gentleness
to assist your mothering today.**

I am gentle and humble in heart,
and you will find rest for your souls.
—Matthew 11:29

271

Work to Play

66 I wish I could be home to play with my baby as much as you are to play with yours," my friend confided. Something felt wrong about the comment, not representative of what was really going on.

It's true that I spend more time at home with my baby than she does. Some days at home, though, I probably don't play with the baby any more than I do on the days I'm at work. It's easy to carry him on my hip without really looking at him while I work around the house. Or I pop a cracker into his mouth to pacify him long enough for me to do one more thing.

No matter how much time I spend at home, I still need to plan real playtime with the baby. It doesn't just happen.

**Babies' work is to play.
Playing is work for mothers, too!**

[The Lord's] delight is not in the strength of the horse,
nor his pleasure in the speed of a runner;
but the Lord takes pleasure in those who fear him.
—Psalm 147:10, 11

Choices

I caught myself, earlier today, seriously concentrating on memorizing a book of Mother Goose nursery rhymes. I figured I'd be able to sing them to my baby better if I didn't have to look at the book the whole time. I smiled to remember that, at the same time, my friend, another mother, was seriously concentrating on radiology in preparation for her doctoral exams next week.

Sometimes I wish my mind were being more challenged and sometimes my friend wishes for less, but we're both choosing to be where we are for now. What a funny and wonderful world, where we can do such different things and both be right!

**Thank God
for the blessings in your current situation.**

And whatever you do, in word or deed,
do everything in the name of the Lord Jesus,
giving thanks to God.

—Colossians 3:17

Stop, Look, and Listen

Today I tried something different. Instead of making my list of things to do and then frantically rushing through the day to do them, I stopped. I asked God to look at the list with me.

Lo and behold, the list took on a strange new perspective. "Making cookies" had been a must, but suddenly it was something that would be nice to do if I had time left over. Shopping could be done tomorrow, and the baby would probably survive without a bath.

My day was transformed into a gift. Chores lost their drudgery. Using the list as a guide, instead of a mandate, freed me to enjoy more than I had thought of in the morning! I even had time to play, which hadn't been on my original list.

Act like you have nothing better to do than play with your baby—because you might not!

> The human mind plans the way,
> but the Lord directs the steps.
>
> —Proverbs 16:9

Flexibility

I've never been good at changing plans, especially if I liked the original plans. I get upset. I sulk. Inside, I feel like a child who can't quit being miserable because she didn't get the bubble gum she wanted. Outside, I don't want anyone else to be happy either.

Now it seems my plans are constantly in flux. My baby spikes a fever and I have to stay home with her for twenty-four hours. She goes to sleep just when I was ready to go shopping. The babysitter forgets to come when I was looking forward all week to a date with my husband. Either this baby is going to change me into a more flexible person, or I will be miserable on a fairly regular basis! I'm amazed again at the influence this tiny person has on who I'm becoming.

**Focus, today,
on what in your life remains stable.**

For I, the Lord, do not change;
therefore you, O children of Jacob, have not perished.
—Malachi 3:6

Contentment

Now I love it when my baby wakens. He doesn't need to eat immediately, like he did when he was younger, but he's not awake enough to venture out on his own yet either. He just lies against me and watches the world from the safety and warmth of my lap.

I like that image of myself, too—sitting in the comfort of God's lap and arms, looking out at the world. I know sometime I will get up again; sometime I'll need to seek nourishment more actively. For now, however, I'll soak in the silence of love.

**Imagine yourself, today,
snuggled into God's arms.**

My soul is like the weaned child that is with me.
—Psalm 131:2

Joy

Nothing out of the ordinary is happening for me, and yet I am flooded with peace. I have accomplished no big thing, but I am bursting with joy. I have no new insights, but everything I see as I move through the day seems to explode into music.

I look at the baby and immediately know the source of my joy. She has made me a mother. One day she will call me "Mom" or maybe "Mama." She has given me this new identity, which I will never give up. Some days that will likely cause me much grief. Today, however, I am entranced by its beauty.

**You are one of many mothers and,
at the same time,
uniquely your child's only mother.**

You shall go out in joy,
and be led back in peace;
the mountains and the hills before you shall burst into song.
—Isaiah 55:12

Ambivalence

Some mothers can't wait until their babies are old enough to talk. They can't wait to hear about their dreams and where it hurts when they cry.

Some mothers don't want their babies to grow up. They hold them constantly so they can't practice walking.

Some mothers can't get enough of their babies. They clang the pots and pans, hoping to shorten a nap that has been going on too long.

Some mothers long for a break from their babies. They wonder when their babies will ever be comfortable living apart from them.

I am, in fact, all of these.

**Notice, today,
your varied dispositions
and what makes you grateful or irritated.**

The Lord will fulfill his purpose for me;
your steadfast love, O Lord, endures forever.
—Psalm 138:8

Hardest Job in the World

Every time I start a new job, I feel overwhelmed. It seems, at first, that this is the hardest thing I've ever done, and I wonder if I'll ever learn everything I need to know to do a good job. Of course, I've always just left a job in which I felt fairly competent at the end, and that feeling soon resumes in the new job as well.

This mothering thing, though, is one I'm beginning to believe I will never master. Every time I think I'm learning how to deal with my child's actions and reactions, she's on to new ones! I've never done so much learning, consultation, repetition, manual labor, basic training, or self-giving on any job before in my life.

I don't care how many others have done it before. Mothering is clearly the hardest job available.

**Remember
that even when you don't have the wisdom
of the Lord, you have the spirit of the Lord.**

The spirit of the Lord God is upon me.

—Isaiah 61:1

Guilt

I'm so tired of feeling guilty about the time I'm gone from my daughter. I try to turn it off like the water faucet when I find it running, but then I wake up and it's running again!

I guess guilt can be constructive if it keeps me from doing what I shouldn't. But no matter how much I try to achieve a good balance between our times together and apart, I always feel guilty about our time apart.

Why does her father, who is gone from her more than I am, not carry the same guilt as I do about it? He would like to be with her more, but he knows he can't so he goes back to work. Guilt doesn't splash all over his life like my leaky faucet. Society has been much kinder to men in that way.

I must learn to claim the boundaries that seem right for us on this effort toward creating a family.

**God, help me discern the difference
between constructive and destructive guilt.**

It is the Lord God who helps me;
who will declare me guilty?
—Isaiah 50:9

Growth

I was so excited when my baby rolled over for the first time. Later when he started creeping across the floor, I couldn't wait to tell everyone. Both times, though, my delight was tempered by a feeling of loss. What a strange combination! Well, maybe not.

Both of these changes happened when I was finally learning what to expect. Suddenly I wasn't certain that if I laid him on the bed, he would be there when I returned. Laying him on a blanket no longer saved him from the dirt on the rest of the floor. I am losing my baby!

God,
if I can't stay ahead of my child,
help me to at least stay caught up.

Just as you do not know how the breath
comes to the bones in the mother's womb,
so you do not know the work of God,
who makes everything.
—Ecclesiastes 11:5

Patience

I always thought of myself as a fairly patient person. But then I never had a child before. I never had my limits stretched this far before—physically, mentally, or emotionally.

Now I realize how much choice I once had in my life. I could sleep all night, read for hours on end, and take lots of time to fix a special meal if I wanted to. If other adults irritated me, I could usually get away from them when I wanted to.

This child is here to stay, for better and for worse, and some rough edges are starting to show up in my personality. I never knew how impatient, irritable, and resentful I could be!

**God,
help me to learn the patience of love,
even when I'm tired,
even when I don't have time to cook or to eat,
and even when my hormones
are controlling my tear ducts.**

Love is patient . . . it is not irritable or resentful.
—I Corinthians 13:4, 5

Boundaries

My tiny, helpless baby has suddenly turned into disaster on the move! I feel like a broken record chanting "No" and a constant companion to redirect his inquisitive mind and fingers.

I struggle with how much to set limits for him and when to let him learn on his own. I hate watching him fall, but I have to let him learn. I wonder if I will eventually have to work as hard to relinquish this job of directing his every move, as I'm now working to learn how to do it.

**God,
help me know when to set boundaries
and when to let my growing child set his own.**

No, my son!
No, son of my womb!
No, son of my vows.

—Proverbs 31:2

Imitation

It's almost scary how much this child is watching everything I do! I had to quit eating popcorn while he's awake because he kept grabbing for it. I quit watching my favorite television show because it suddenly didn't seem like such a good thing for his little eyes to see. He even tries to comb his hair like he's seen me use the comb.

I've never been such a central role model for anyone before. It's flattering—and overwhelming with responsibility. I guess that's part of what I asked for when I invited him into my life.

**God,
help me deserve his eyes.**

My child, give me your heart,
and let your eyes observe my ways.
—Proverbs 23:26

Growing Pains

I'll have to admit, one of the things I was eager to experience with a baby was having someone who loves me more than anyone else. When I was little, babies always cried when I held them. I longed to have one who stopped crying when I picked her up, one for whom I was the best comfort.

Well, I got what I wanted—but overdone! Sometimes I would like to be able to talk on the phone without her screaming for my attention. I'd like it if someone else could comfort her when I'm busy making supper. And I hate leaving her when my last image is of her arms reaching desperately for me, her eyes filled with tears.

With the privilege of being loved exclusively comes a harder task. I have to prove to her that, even though I am not always available, she can trust me to return.

I cannot be everything for my child. God, help my baby and me both to cope with that reality.

The girl went and called the child's mother.
—Exodus 2:8

Losing Control

When I decided to get married, I knew I'd have to give up some of the control I had in my life. I'd probably have to stop reading while I ate supper. Journaling time might yield to more conversational time. My husband might not be thrilled about my working the midnight shift at the shelter for homeless women.

I feel like I got married all over again this year. Not only do I not read during supper, I often don't have time to eat it either. Journaling time is history, and I have to take an early evening nap when I work the midnight shift!

But then after everyone else is sleeping for the night, I notice a tiny pair of shoes lined up beside two big pairs at the door, and I smile. She's here to stay, and I wouldn't want it any other way.

**Give your baby
some special "honeymoon" time today.**

[Love] bears all things, believes all things,
hopes all things, endures all things.
—I Corinthians 13:7

Childhood Memory

It was a particular look I saw in the baby's eyes. I don't know what was happening inside him, but the look flashed back a vivid memory to me that I hadn't thought about in years. With his look, I remembered a joy that exploded inside of me and pushed me into my dad's arms when he returned from a trip one afternoon.

What a powerful revisitation! Growing with my child just may allow me to relive my childhood all over again!

**God,
prepare me for the renewal
of my childhood joys and pain
that I've invited by entering parenthood.**

Remember the days of old,
consider the years long past.
—Deuteronomy 32:7

Separation Anxiety

It was so awful trying to leave my baby with a friend. As soon as she knew we were leaving, she started crying and gripped my neck. We finally had to just leave.

The whole way to the concert I wondered if John and I really needed this evening alone. Couldn't I be a good spouse without also abandoning my child? Her screams in my head drowned out most of the music I paid to hear. Forget the dessert, I just wanted to go home and hold my crying baby.

Upon our return, however, the writhing child in my head was sleeping peacefully. "We had a great time," our friend said. "She quit crying as soon as you closed the door." When will I believe that in time to enjoy our evening out?

Practice inner peace.

Go in peace.

—Luke 8:48

291

Emotional Seesaw

Along with this relatively new role of motherhood comes a recurring voice. It asks, "What makes you think you could take on such a big responsibility?"

I shrink in the face of this question and can only reply, "I don't know! Maybe I made a mistake." Then my baby's eyes light up when I walk into her room. She reaches for me. She nestles into my shoulder. I feel like a mother.

Will I be on this seesaw all my life? Maybe I can learn to trust that God is on the other end of the board and will keep pushing me back up again.

**Entertain just enough doubt
in your own capabilities to
require your reliance on God.**

I can do all things through him [Christ]
who strengthens me.

—Philippians 4:13

Crying

Before I had a baby, I remember people telling me that babies have lots of different cries and I would learn what each one meant. That was hard to believe, because a cry was a cry to me, and I hated hearing all of them!

Here we are, though, well into his first year, and I suddenly remembered those words. Sure enough, the miracle seems so ordinary now. I know his hungry cry from his sleepy cry, his "I want to be held" cry from his "Change my diaper NOW" cry. Today I heard a new one. I put his vitamin bottle out of his reach and he let out a mad cry! I laughed. Now I feel like a real mother!

**Thank you, God,
for creating babies with such a
variety of communication skills.**

He was crying,
and she took pity on him.

—Exodus 2:6

293

Good Mother

"**Y**ou're a good mother!"

I heard the words directed at me, but I couldn't muster an acceptable response. All I could think of were the times I've failed. Sometimes I forget to change his diaper for hours, and he gets a rash on his bottom. Too often I stick him in the backpack so I can get my work done instead of playing with him. Just this morning I left him crying in his crib for ten minutes while I finished talking to Anne on the phone.

On the other hand, I do play with him a lot. I try to see that he gets home to nap on schedule most of the time. I do put some effort into keeping him fairly clean and well nourished.

After a long moment, I said, "Thank you."

**Receive the compliments of others
without dissecting the joy out of them!**

My steadfast love shall not depart from you,
and my covenant of peace shall not be removed,
says the Lord.

—Isaiah 54:10

Miracle of Life

When my baby was first born, I spent hours watching her. Every twist of her mouth, raise of an eyebrow, or movement of a tiny finger made me smile. Instead of laying her down when she went to sleep in my arms, I treasured her peaceful face and relaxed body.

The day after her birth, I found it hard to imagine that hers was the heartbeat I heard through the monitor. This is the being responsible for all those kicks and jabs under my ribs. This person had been floating around in her own little oblivion only hours before.

After many months I still catch myself watching her intensely—in awe. Can she really have once been inside me?

God,
thank you for letting me help you create this life.

You knit me together in my mother's womb.

—Psalm 139:13

Returning Energy

The process of getting my baby to give up his early morning feeding was not fun, but the end results are wonderful! I almost forgot what it was like to sleep as long as the sun! I don't think he was really hungry anymore at five-thirty every morning. He had just gotten used to our getting up together for ten minutes so I could put him back to sleep. He cried for a few days when he didn't get his snack, but now we are both enjoying an extra two hours of uninterrupted sleep.

This morning I actually got up before his cry made me do it! He looked so peaceful, and I was definitely more rested. This mother-son team is getting better all the time.

**Thank God for the quiet,
steady return of energy.**

I have calmed and quieted my soul,
like a weaned child with its mother.

—Psalm 131:2

297

Self-Reflection

I can already see traits in my baby that mimic her mother's! She loves to laugh, and she brightens up when we have guests. The more we have, the merrier the day! Of course I'm conscious of only the things I like about myself in her.

I'm sure she will also mirror the parts of myself I'd rather not look at. Our similarities will probably cause our biggest clashes. Accepting my daughter as she grows may depend on how well I accept myself—especially the undesirable features!

Lord,
help me to love myself,
and, in turn,
better love my child.

Love your neighbor as yourself.
—Romans 13:9

On the Move

All of a sudden I'm looking at our house in a new way, and it has got to change. Last week it was fine, but this week it's a long way from being childproof. This previously sedentary bundle has, without warning, gone into high gear.

I guess this is the stage where my extra pounds come off. I'm constantly with him, either clearing the path before him of inedible objects or chasing after him to pick up the pieces. It's both delightful and exhausting!

I find it a comical, comforting thought to consider how like this baby I must be in the eyes of my Creator. It makes sense that God does not go far from me!

**Ponder from what calamities
you have likely been protected.**

God is not far from us . . . we are his offspring.
—Acts 17:27, 28

Lack of Focus

I constantly scurry around, trying to do so many things at once that I fear I'm losing my ability to concentrate on one thing at a time. It hit me last Sunday at the end of the worship service. I haven't heard any of the sermons I've sat through for almost a year now . . . yes, I think I can trace it back to the birth of the baby.

I can make dinner and pick strawberries with a baby on my hip. I have cut out and organized coupons while making my grocery list, while giving my child a bath, while drying my hair. I regularly pick up toys on the way to changing a diaper, as supper boils on the stove and I'm telling my husband on the phone what to buy on his way home.

Yes, my skill at doing everything at once is perfected. Now for sharpening my ability to focus!

**Try doing only one thing for five minutes.
Set a timer;
it may feel like an hour!**

For those who desire life and desire to see good days . . .
let them seek peace and pursue it.
—I Peter 3:10, 11

Redefining My World

Sometimes I reflect with fascination on how I'm changing. Tonight I was very comfortable asking the hostess of the party if she had any juice, even though only soda and coffee were being served. I didn't wait for an official tour of the house to find the toy room.

For the comfort and happiness of my child, I have taken up behavior that once seemed rude and pushy. I notice other parents feeling free to do the same in my home. Children redefine the world, and I like how that loosens things up!

Thank you, God,
for how the presence of a child
is smoothing my rigid rules of life.

Taking [a child] in his arms,
[Jesus] said to them,
"Whoever welcomes one such child
in my name welcomes me."
—Mark 9:36, 37

Changing Patterns

One of my friends who was abused as a child sees the evil of how she was treated in fresh ways now that she has children of her own. She knows that no child deserves to be treated like she was. She also knows how difficult it is not to repeat those patterns when abusive reactions from adults are what she expected for years, and would be natural for her to replicate.

I already hear myself telling my baby direct recordings that are lodged in my head from my parents. They aren't necessarily bad, but I want to give energy and thought to deciding what attitudes and actions I will perpetuate and what I will change.

**Thank you,
Jesus, for the vision and strength you lend to
help me make choices about how to be a mother.**

So if anyone is in Christ,
there is a new creation: everything old has passed away;
see, everything has become new.

— II Corinthians 5:17

303

Busy

On my busy days I try to remember a story that one of my teachers told me years ago. He said that he was prone to complaining about how busy his life had become. He longed aloud for more time to relax, until the day his wife picked up his datebook and calmly observed, "That's funny. All these appointments were made in your handwriting."

**You have choices
about how to use your time.
Let that knowledge empower your decisions.**

It is God's gift that all should eat and drink
and take pleasure in all their toil.

—Ecclesiastes 3:13

Mess Is Normal

Today I felt like a real mother. A new babysitter was over for a few hours and offered to stay longer, for free, to help clean up the mess. I looked around and didn't see it! It looked like a normal day's activity center.

I mumbled something about reading that you shouldn't clean up too much, or your child will think she's not supposed to play, and shooed her out the door. She had just enough time to say she was recanting her desire for children.

I had to laugh. I would have said the same thing a year ago.

**If you don't already have one,
make a "Bless This Mess" motto
to place in your home,
or at least to hang around your heart.**

Jesus said, "Let the little children come to me,
and do not stop them;
for it is to such as these that the
kingdom of heaven belongs."
—Matthew 19:14

How Many Children?

When we first talked about having a child, my husband wasn't sure he had enough energy to give to another primary relationship. I've always had enough energy for as many friends as I could find; for me it was more a question of whether or not I wanted to give up time from all my other interests to be a parent.

Now that Maria has taken up residency in our home, full of demands and love, often with the voting power of two, I can see how much she surprised both of us. Her move into our lives has taken less energy than John expected and more than I was prepared for.

Every once in a while, though, we think about giving her a sibling. Amazingly, our inner natures express themselves in full force. I say, "Two can't be any more work than one, since one already takes all of my time." John says, "Three primary relationships in the same household! I don't know . . ." Oh well, we don't have to decide today.

Give me wisdom, Lord,
as I make decisions about the
"ifs" and "whens" of more children.

Be fruitful and multiply.

—Genesis 9:1